EVERYMAN,
I WILL GO WITH THEE
AND BE THY GUIDE,
IN THY MOST NEED
TO GO BY THY SIDE

EVERYMAN'S LIBRARY
POCKET POETS

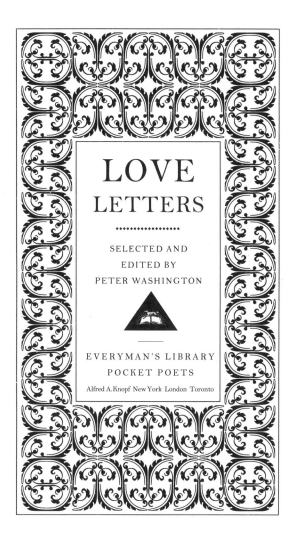

LOVE
LETTERS

••••••••••••••••••

SELECTED AND
EDITED BY
PETER WASHINGTON

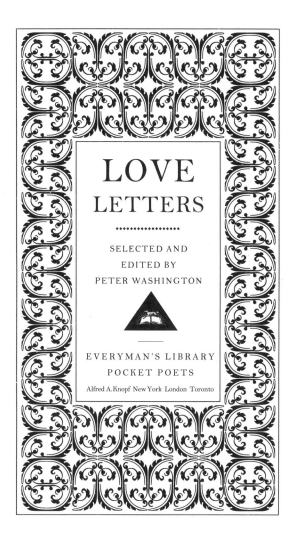

EVERYMAN'S LIBRARY
POCKET POETS

Alfred A. Knopf   New York London Toronto

THIS IS A BORZOI BOOK
PUBLISHED BY ALFRED A. KNOPF

This selection by Peter Washington first published in
Everyman's Library, 1996
Copyright © 1996 by Everyman's Library

Thirteenth printing (US)

A list of acknowledgments to copyright owners appears at the back of
this volume.

All rights reserved. Published in the United States by Alfred A. Knopf,
a division of Random House, Inc., New York, and in Canada by Random
House of Canada Limited, Toronto. Distributed by Random House, Inc.,
New York. Published in the United Kingdom by Everyman's Library,
Northburgh House, 10 Northburgh Street, London EC1V 0AT.
Distributed by Random House (UK) Ltd.

US website: www.randomhouse.com/everymans

ISBN 978-0-679-44689-7 (US)
978-1-85715-726-0 (UK)

A CIP catalogue record for this book is available from the British Library

Typography by Peter B. Willberg
Typeset in the UK by AccComputing, North Barrow, Somerset
Printed and bound in Germany by GGP Media GmbH, Pössneck

CONTENTS

5

INTOXICATION

ADORATION

SEPARATION

INSTRUCTION

REFLECTION

CONFESSION

ABOUT LETTERS

Here are the dear letters.

Stella Campbell to Bernard Shaw

Love is a talkative passion.

Bishop Wilson

INVITATION

Ann Hamilton and Barbara Villiers to Lord
Chesterfield   1657

My Lord,

My friend and I are now abed together a-contriving
how to have your company this afternoon. If you
deserve this favour, you will come and seek us at
Ludgate Hill about three a clock at Butler's shop, where
we will expect you, but lest we should give you too
much satisfaction at once, we will say no more; expect
the rest when you see

Your &c

Alfred de Musset to George Sand   [1833]

My dear George,

I have something stupid and ridiculous to tell you. I
am foolishly writing you instead of telling you this, I do
not know why, when returning from that walk. To-
night I shall be annoyed at having done so. You will
laugh in my face, will take me for a phrase-maker in all
my relations with you hitherto. You will show me the
door and you will think I am lying. I am in love with
you.

Alfred de Musset

George Farquhar to Anne Oldfield
Sunday, after Sermon [1699?]

I came, I saw, and was conquered; never had man more
to say, yet can I say nothing; where others go to save
their souls, there have I lost mine; but I hope that
Divinity which has the justest title to its service has
received it; but I will endeavour to suspend these
raptures for a moment, and talk calmly. –

Nothing on earth, madam, can charm, beyond your
wit but your beauty: after this not to love you would
proclaim me a fool; and to say I did when I thought
otherwise would pronounce me a knave; if anybody
called me either I should resent it; and if you but think
me either I shall break my heart.

You have already, madam, seen enough of me to
create a liking or an aversion; your sense is above your
sex, then let your proceeding be so likewise, and tell
me plainly what I have to hope for. Were I to consult
my merits my humility would chide any shadow of
hope; but after a sight of such a face whose whole
composition is a smile of good nature, why should I be
so unjust as to suspect you of cruelty. Let me either
live in *London* and be happy or retire again to my
desert to check my vanity that drew me thence; but let
me beg you to receive my sentence from your own
mouth, that I may hear you speak and see you look

at the same time; then let me be unfortunate if I can.

If you are not the lady in mourning that sat upon my right hand at church, you may go to the devil, for I'm sure you're a witch.

Laurence Sterne to Lady P(ercy)
Mount Coffee-House, Tuesday, 3 o'clock [1765?]

There is a strange mechanical effect produced in writing a billet-doux within a stonecast of the lady who engrosses the heart and soul of an inamorato – for this cause (but mostly because I am to dine in this neighbourhood) have I, Tristram Shandy, come forth from my lodgings to a coffee-house the nearest I could find to my dear Lady —'s house, and have called for a sheet of gilt paper, to try the truth of this article of my creed. Now for it –

O my dear lady – what a dishclout of a soul hast thou made of me? I think, by the bye, this is a little too familiar an introduction, for so unfamiliar a situation as I stand in with you – where heaven knows, I am kept at a distance – and despair of getting one inch nearer you, with all the steps and windings I can think of to recommend myself to you. Would not any man in his senses run diametrically from you – and as far as his legs would carry him, rather than thus causelessly, foolishly, and foolhardily expose himself afresh – and afresh, where his heart and reason tells him he shall be sure to come off loser, if not totally undone? Why would you tell me you would be glad to see me? Does it give you pleasure to make me more unhappy – or does it add to your triumph, that your eyes and lips have turned a man into a fool, whom the rest of the town is courting as a wit? I am a fool – the weakest, the most ductile, the most tender fool that ever woman tried the weakness of – and the most unsettled in my purposes and resolutions of recovering my right mind. It is but an hour ago, that I kneeled down and swore I never would come near you – and after saying my Lord's Prayer for the sake of the close, *of not being led into temptation* – out I sallied like any Christian hero, ready to take the field against the world, the flesh, and the devil; not doubting but I should finally trample them all down under my feet. And now I am got so near you – within this vile stone's cast of your house – I feel myself drawn into a vortex, that has turned my brain upside downwards; and though I had purchased a box ticket to carry me to Miss *******'s benefit, yet I know very well, that was a single line directed to me to let me know Lady — would be alone at seven, and suffer me to spend the evening with her, she would infallibly see every thing verified I have told her. I dine at Mr C — r's in Wigmore-street, in this neigh-bourhood, where I shall stay till seven, in hopes you purpose to put me to this proof. If I hear nothing by that time, I shall conclude you are better disposed of – and shall take a sorry hack, and sorrily jog on to the play. Curse on the word. I know nothing but sorrow – except this one thing, that I love you (perhaps foolishly, but)

most sincerely,

L. Sterne

Jane Clairmont to Lord Byron   *1815*

You bid me write short to you and I have much to say. You also bade me believe that it was a fancy which made me cherish an attachment for you. It cannot be a fancy since you have been for the last year the object upon which every solitary moment led me to muse.

I do not expect you to love me, I am not worthy of your love. I feel you are superior, yet much to my surprise, more to my happiness, you betrayed passions I had believed no longer alive in your bosom. Shall I also have to ruefully experience the want of happiness? Shall I reject it when it is offered? I may appear to you imprudent, vicious; my opinions detestable, my theory depraved; but one thing, at least, time shall show you: that I love gently and with affection, that I am incapable of anything approaching to the feeling of revenge or malice; I do assure you, your future will shall be mine, and everything you shall do or say, I shall not question.

Have you then any objection to the following plan? On Thursday Evening we may go out of town together by some stage or mail about the distance of ten or twelve miles. There we shall be free and unknown; we can return early the following morning. I have arranged every thing here so that the slightest suspicion may not be excited. Pray do so with your people.

Will you admit me for two moments to settle with you where? Indeed I will not stay an instant after you tell me to go. Only so much may be said and done in a short time by an interview which writing cannot effect. Do what you will, or go where you will, refuse to see me and behave unkindly, I shall never forget you. I shall ever remember the gentleness of your manners and the wild originality of your countenance. Having been once seen, you are not to be forgotten. Perhaps this is the last time I shall ever address you. Once more, then, let me assure you that I am not ungrateful. In all things have you acted most honourably, and I am only provoked that the awkwardness of my manner and something like timidity has hitherto prevented my expressing it to you personally.

Clara Clairmont

Will you admit me now as I wait in Hamilton Place for your answer?

Robert Browning to Elizabeth Barrett
Friday, 10 January 1845

I love your verses with all my heart, dear Miss Barrett,
– and this is no offhand complimentary letter that I shall
write, – whatever else, no prompt matter-of-course
recognition of your genius and there a graceful and
natural end of the thing: since the day last week when
I first read your poems, I quite laugh to remember how I
have been turning and turning again in my mind what
I should be able to tell you of their effect upon me – for
in the first flush of delight I thought I would this once
get out of my habit of purely passive enjoyment, when I
do really enjoy, and thoroughly justify my admiration –
perhaps even, as a loyal fellowcraftsman should, try and
find fault and do you some little good to be proud of
hereafter! – but nothing comes of it all – so into me has it
gone, and part of me has it become, this great living
poetry of yours, not a flower of which but took root and
grew – oh, how different that is from lying to be dried
and pressed flat and prized highly and put in a book
with a proper account at top and bottom, and shut up
and put away ... and the book called a 'Flora', besides!
After all I need not give up the thought of doing that,
too, in time; because even now, talking with whoever is
worthy, I can give a reason for my faith in one and
another excellence, the fresh strange music, the affluent

language, the exquisite pathos and true new brave thought – but in this addressing myself to you, your own self, and for the first time, my feeling rises altogether. I do, as I say, love these books with all my heart – and I love you too: do you know I was once not very far from seeing – really seeing you? Mr Kenyon said to me one morning would you like to see Miss Barrett? – then he went to announce me, – then he returned ... you were too unwell – and now it is years ago – and I feel as at some untoward passage in my travels – as if I had been close, so close, to some world's-wonder in chapel or crypt, only a screen to push and I might have entered, but there was some slight ... so it now seems ... slight and just-sufficient bar to admission, and the half-opened door shut, and I went home my thousands of miles, and the sight was never to be!

Well, these Poems were to be – and this true thankful joy and pride with which I feel myself

Yours ever faithfully,

Robert Browning

Elizabeth Barrett to Robert Browning
Saturday, January 1845

I thank you, dear Mr Browning, from the bottom of my heart. You meant to give me pleasure by your letter – and even if the object had not been answered, I ought still to thank you. But it is thoroughly answered. Such a letter from such a hand! Sympathy is dear – very dear to me: but the sympathy of a poet & of such a poet, is the quintessence of sympathy to me! Will you take back my gratitude for it? – agreeing too that of all the commerce done in the world, from Tyre to Carthage, the exchange of sympathy for gratitude is the most princely thing?

For the rest you draw me on with your kindness. It is difficult to get rid of people when you once have given them too much pleasure – that is a fact, & we will not stop for the moral of it. What I was going to say ... after a little-natural hesitation ... is, that if ever you emerge without inconvenient effort from your 'passive state', & will tell me of such faults as rise to the surface & strike you as important in my poems (for of course, I do not think of troubling you with criticism in detail) – you will confer a lasting obligation on me, and one which I shall value so much, that I covet it at a distance. I do not pretend to any extraordinary meekness under criticism – and it is possible enough that I might not be altogether obedient to yours. But with my high respect for your power in your Art, your experience as an artist, it would be quite impossible for me to hear a general observation of yours on what appear to you my master-faults, without being the better for it hereafter in some way. I ask for only a sentence or two of general observation – and I do not ask even for that, so as to teaze you – but in the humble, low voice, which is so excellent a thing in women – particularly when they go a-begging. The most frequent general criticism I receive, is I think, upon the style ... 'if I would but change my style!' – But that is an objection (isn't it?) to the writer bodily? Buffon says, and every sincere writer must feel, that 'Le style *c'est l'homme* – a fact, however, scarcely calculated to lessen the objection with certain critics. –

Is it indeed true that I was so near to the pleasure and honour of making your acquaintance? – and can it be true that you look back upon the lost opportunity with any regret? – But, ... you know ... if you had entered the 'crypt', you might have caught cold, or been tired to death, & wished yourself 'a thousand miles off' – which wd have been worse than travelling them. It is not my interest however to put such thoughts in your head about its being 'all for the best' – and I would rather hope (as I do) that what I lost by one chance I may recover by some future one. Winters shut me up as they do a dormouse's eyes: in the spring, we shall see & I am so much better that I seem turning round to the outward world again. And in the meantime I have learnt to know your voice, not merely from the poetry but from the kindness in it.

I am writing too much, notwithstanding, – and notwithstanding that I am writing too much, I will write of one thing more. I will say that I am your debtor, not only for this cordial letter & for all the pleasure which came with it, but in other ways, & those the highest: & I will say that while I live to follow this divine art of poetry, . . . in proportion to my love for it & my devotion to it, I must be a devout admirer & student of your works. This is in my heart to say to you & I say it.

And, for the rest, I am proud to remain
Your obliged & faithful
Elizabeth B. Barrett

Franz Kafka to Felice Bauer   *11 November 1912*

Fräulein Felice!

I am now going to ask you a favour which sounds quite crazy, and which I should regard as such, were I the one to receive the letter. It is also the very greatest test that even the kindest person could be put to. Well, this is it:

Write to me only once a week, so that your letter arrives on Sunday – for I cannot endure your daily letters, I am incapable of enduring them. For instance, I answer one of your letters, then lie in bed in apparent calm, but my heart beats through my entire body and is conscious only of you. I belong to you; there is really no other way of expressing it, and that is not strong enough. But for this very reason I don't want to know what you are wearing; it confuses me so much that I cannot deal with life; and that's why I don't want to know that you are fond of me. If I did, how could I, fool that I am, go on sitting in my office, or here at home, instead of leaping on to a train with my eyes shut and opening them only when I am with you? Oh, there is a sad, sad reason for not doing so. To make it short: my health is only just good enough for myself alone, not good enough for marriage, let alone fatherhood. Yet when I read your letter, I feel I could overlook even what cannot possibly be overlooked.

If only I had your answer now! And how horribly I torment you, and how I compel you, in the stillness of your room, to read this letter, as nasty a letter as has ever lain on your desk! Honestly, it strikes me sometimes that I prey like a spectre on your felicitous name! If only I had mailed Saturday's letter, in which I implored you never to write to me again, and in which I gave a similar promise. Oh God, what prevented me from sending that letter? All would be well. But is a peaceful solution possible now? Would it help if we wrote to each other only once a week? No, if my suffering could be cured by such means it would not be serious. And already I foresee that I shan't be able to endure even the Sunday letters. And so, to compensate for Saturday's lost opportunity, I ask you with what energy remains to me at the end of this letter: if we value our lives, let us abandon it all.

Did I think of signing myself *Dein*? No, nothing could be more false. No, I am forever fettered to myself, that's what I am, and that's what I must try to live with.

Franz

Stella Campbell to Bernard Shaw   18th November 1912

33 Kensington Square

No more shams – a real love letter this time – then I can breathe freely, and perhaps who knows begin to sit up and get well –

I haven't said 'kiss me' because life is too short for the kiss my heart calls for ... All your words are as idle wind – Look into my eyes for two minutes without speaking if you dare! Where would be your 54 years? and my grandmothers heart? and how many hours would you be late for dinner?

— If you give me one kiss and you can only kiss me if I say 'kiss me' and I will never say 'kiss me' because I am a respectable widow and I wouldn't let any man kiss me unless I was sure of the wedding ring –

Stella (Liza, I mean).

Margery Brews to John Paston *[February 1477]*

To my right well-beloved cousin, John Paston, Esquire, be this letter delivered, etc.

Right worshipful and well-beloved Valentine, in my most humble wise I recommend me unto you, etc. And heartily I thank you for the letter which that ye sent me by John Bickerton, whereby I understand and know that ye be purposed to come to Topcroft in short time, and without any errand or matter but only to have a conclusion of the matter betwixt my father and you. I would be most glad of any creature alive, so that the matter might grow to effect. And thereas ye say, an' ye come and find the matter no more towards you than ye did aforetime, ye would no more put my father and my lady my mother to no cost nor business for that cause a good while after; which causeth mine heart to be full heavy. And if that ye come, and the matter take to none effect, then should I be much more sorry and full of heaviness.

And as for myself, I have done and understood in the matter that I can or may, as God knoweth; and I let you plainly understand that my father will no more money part withal in that behalf, but £100 and 50 marks, which is right far from the accomplishment of your desire.

Wherefore, if that ye could be content with that good and my poor person, I would be the merriest maiden on ground. And if ye think not yourself so satisfied, or that ye might have much more good (as I have understood by you afore) – good, true, and loving Valentine, that ye take no such labour upon you as to come more for that matter, but let it pass, and never more to be spoken of, as I may be your true lover and beadswoman during my life.

No more unto you at this time, but Almighty Jesus preserve you both body and soul, etc.

By your Valentine,

Margery Brews

King Henry VIII to Anne Boleyn   *[c. 1528]*

In debating with myself the contents of your letters I have been put to a great agony; not knowing how to understand them, whether to my disadvantage as shown in some places, or to my advantage as in others. I beseech you now with all my heart definitely to let me know your whole mind as to the love between us; for necessity compels me to plague you for a reply, having been for more than a year now struck by the dart of love, and being uncertain either of failure or of finding a place in your heart and affection, which point has certainly kept me for some time from naming you my mistress, since if you only love me with an ordinary love the name is not appropriate to you, seeing that it stands for an uncommon position very remote from the ordinary; but if it pleases you to do the duty of a true, loyal mistress and friend, and to give yourself body and heart to me, who have been, and will be, your very loyal servant (if your rigour does not forbid me), I promise you that not only the name will be due to you, but also to take you as my sole mistress, casting off all others than yourself out of mind and affection, and to serve you only; begging you to make me a complete reply to this my rude letter as to how far and in what I can trust; and if it does not please you to reply in writing, to let me know of some place where I can have it by word of mouth, the which place I will seek out with all my heart. No more for fear of wearying you. Written by the hand of him who would willingly remain your

HR

Tell you what you might do while you are alone at Pixton. You might think about me a bit & whether, if those wop priests ever come to a decent decision, you could bear the idea of marrying me. Of course you haven't got to decide, but think about it. I can't advise you in my favour because I think it would be beastly for you, but think how nice it would be for me. I am restless & moody & misanthropic & lazy & have no money except what I earn and if I got ill you would starve. In fact its a lousy proposition. On the other hand I think I could do a Grant and reform & become quite strict about not getting drunk and I am pretty sure I should be faithful. Also there is always a fair chance that there will be another bigger economic crash in which case if you had married a nobleman with a great house you might find yourself starving, while I am very clever and could probably earn a living of some sort somewhere. Also though you would be taking on an elderly buffer, I am one without fixed habits. You wouldn't find yourself confined to any particular place or group. Also I have practically no living relatives except one brother whom I scarcely know. You would not find yourself involved in a large family & all their rows & you would not be patronized & interfered with by odious sisters in law & aunts as often happens. All these are very small advantages compared with the awfulness of my character. I have always tried to be nice to you and you may have got it into your head that I am nice really, but that is all rot. It is only to you & for you. I am jealous & impatient – but there is no point in going into a whole list of my vices. You are a critical girl and I've no doubt that you know them all and a great many I don't know myself. But the point I wanted to make is that if you marry most people, you are marrying a great number of objects & other people as well, well if you marry me there is nothing else involved, and that is an advantage as well as a disadvantage. My only tie of any kind is my work. That means that for several months each year we shall have to separate or you would have to share some very lonely place with me. But apart from that we could do what we liked & go where we liked – and if you married a soldier or stockbroker or member of parliament or master of hounds you would be more tied. When I tell my friends that I am in love with a girl of 19 they looked shocked and say 'wretched child' but I dont look on you as very young even in your beauty and I dont think there is any sense in the line that you cannot possibly commit yourself to a decision that affects your whole life for years yet. But anyway there is no point in your deciding or even answering. I may never get free of your cousin Evelyn. Above all things, darling, dont fret at all. But just turn the matter over in your dear head.

... I am looking over the sea and endeavouring to reckon up the estate I have to offer you. As far as I can make out my equipment for starting on a journey to fairyland consists of the following items.

1st. A Straw Hat. The oldest part of this admirable relic shows traces of pure Norman work. The vandalism of Cromwell's soldiers has left us little of the original hat-band.

2nd. A Walking Stick, very knobby and heavy: admirably fitted to break the head of any denizen of Suffolk who denies that you are the noblest of ladies, but of no other manifest use.

3rd. A copy of Walt Whitman's poems, once nearly given to Salter, but quite forgotten. It has his name in it still with an affectionate inscription from his sincere friend Gilbert Chesterton. I wonder if he will ever have it.

4th. A number of letters from a young lady, containing everything good and generous and loyal and holy and wise that isn't in Walt Whitman's poems.

5th. An unwieldy sort of a pocket knife, the blades mostly having an edge of a more varied and picturesque outline than is provided by the prosaic cutler. The chief element however is a thing 'to take stones out of a horse's hoof'. What a beautiful sensation of security it gives one to reflect that if one should ever have money enough to buy a horse and should happen to buy one and the horse should happen to have a stone in his hoof – that one is ready; one stands prepared, with a defiant smile!

6th.   Passing from the last miracle of practical foresight, we come to a box of matches. Every now and then I strike one of these, because fire is beautiful and burns your fingers. Some people think this waste of matches: the same people who object to the building of Cathedrals.

7th.   About three pounds in gold and silver, the remains of one of Mr Unwin's bursts of affection: those explosions of spontaneous love for myself, which, such is the perfect order and harmony of his mind, occur at startlingly exact intervals of time.

8th.   A book of Children's Rhymes, in manuscript, called the 'Weather Book' about $\frac{3}{4}$ finished, and destined for Mr Nutt. I have been working at it fairly steadily, which I think jolly creditable under the circumstances. One can't put anything interesting in it. They'll understand those things when they grow up.

9th.   A tennis racket – nay, start not. It is a part of the new regime, and the only new and neat-looking thing in the Museum. We'll soon mellow it – like the straw hat. My brother and I are teaching each other lawn tennis.

10th.   A soul, hitherto idle and omnivorous but now happy enough to be ashamed of itself.

11th.   A body, equally idle and quite equally omnivorous, absorbing tea, coffee, claret, sea-water and oxygen to its own perfect satisfaction. It is happiest swimming, I think, the sea being a convenient size.

12th.   A Heart – mislaid somewhere. And that is about all the property of which an inventory can be made at present. After all, my tastes are stoically simple. A straw hat, a stick, a box of matches and some of his own poetry. What more does man require? . . .

Jane Baillie Welsh to Thomas Carlyle   16 September 1823

My dear Friend,

Your letter only reached me this morning, having sojourned at Templand more than ten days, 'expecting an opportunity' – Charming as it is, I could almost wish it had not cast up at all; for it has troubled me more than I can tell – I feel there is need I should answer it without delay – And what can I say to you? it is so hard to explain one's self in such a situation! but I must! and in plain terms; for any reserve at present were criminal and might be very fatal in its consequences to both –

You misunderstand me – you regard me no longer as a friend, a sister; but as one who at some future period may be more to you than both – is it not so? is it not true that you believe me, like the bulk of my silly sex, incapable of entertaining a strong affection for a man of my own age without having for it's ultimate object our union for life? 'Useless and dangerous to love you'! 'my happiness wrecked by you'! – I cannot have misinterpreted your meaning! And my God what have I said or done to mislead you into an error so destructive to the confidence that subsist[s] betwixt us, so dangerous to the peace of us both? In my treatment of you I have indeed disregarded all maxims of womanly prudence, have shaken myself free from the shackles of etiquette – I have loved and admired you for your noble qualities, and for the extraordinary affection you have shewn me: and I have told you so without reserve or disguise – but *not* till our repeated quarrels had produced an explanation betwixt us, which I foolishly believed would gauruntee my future conduct from all possibility of misconstruction – I have been to blame – I might have foreseen that such implicite confidence might mislead you as to the nature of my sentiments, and should have expressed my friendship for you with a more prudent reserve – but it is of no use talking of what I might or should have done in the time past – I have only to repair the mischief in as far as I can, now that my eyes are opened to it now that I am startled to find our relation actually assuming the aspect of an engagement for life –

My Friend I love you – I repeat it tho' I find the e[x]pression a rash one – all the best feelings of my nature are concerned in loving you – But were you my Brother I would love you the same, were I married to another I would love you the same – and is this sentiment so calm, so delightful – but so unimpassioned enough to recompense the freedom of my heart, enough to reconcile me to the existence of a married woman the hopes and wishes and ambitions of which are all different from mine, the cares and occupations of which are my disgust – Oh no! Your Friend I will be, your truest most devoted friend, while I breath[e] the breath of life; but your wife! never never! Not though you were as rich as Croesus, as honoured and renowned as you yet shall be –

You may think I am viewing the matter by much too seriously – taking fright where there is noth[ing] to fear – It is well if it be so! But, suffering as I am at this very moment from the horrid pain of seeing a true and affectionate heart near breaking for my sake, it is not to be wondered at tho' I be overanxious for your peace on which my own depends in a still greater degree – Write to me and reassure me – for God's sake reassure me if you can! Your Friendship at this time is almost neces-sary to my existence. Yet I will resign it cost what it may – will, will resign it if it can only be enjoyed at the risk of your future peace –

I had many things to say to you – about Musæus and all that, but I must wait till another opportunity – At present I scarcely know what I am about –

Ever Affectionately Yours

Jane B. Welsh

FLIRTATION

Laurence Sterne to Mrs H.   Coxwould, 12 October 1767

Ever since my dear H. wrote me word she was mine, more than ever woman was, I have been racking my memory to inform me where it was that you and I had that affair together. People think that I have had many, some in body, some in mind, but as I told you before, you have had me more than any woman – therefore you must have had me, [Hannah], both in mind, and in body. Now I cannot recollect where it was, nor exactly when – it could not be the lady in Bond-street, or Grosvenor-street, or — Square, or Pall Mall. We shall make it out, H., when we meet. I impatiently long for it – 'tis no matter. I cannot now stand writing to you to-day. I will make it up next post – for dinner is upon table, and if I make Lord F — stay, he will not frank this. How do you do? Which parts of *Tristram* do you like best? God bless you.

> Yours,
>
> L. Sterne

Mozart to his wife   Vienna, 6 June 1791

I have this moment received your dear letter and am delighted to hear that you are well and in good spirits. Madame Leutgeb has laundered my nightcap and necktie, but I should like you to see them! Good God! I kept on telling her, *'Do let me show you how she (my wife) does them!'* – But it was no use. I am delighted that you have a good appetite – but whoever gorges a lot, must also shit a lot – no, walk a lot, I mean. But I should not like you to take *long walks* without me. I entreat you to follow my advice exactly, for it comes from my heart. Adieu – my love – my only one. Do catch them in the air – those 2999½ little kisses from me which are flying about, waiting for someone to snap them up. Listen, I want to whisper something in your ear – and you in mine – and now we open and close our mouths – again – again and again – at last we say: 'It is all about Plumpi – Strumpi –' Well, you can think what you like – that is just why it's so convenient. Adieu. A thousand tender kisses. Ever your

Mozart

Alexander Pope to Teresa Blount   Bath, September [1714]

Madam,

I write to you for two reasons, one is because you commanded it, which will be always a reason to me in anything; the other, because I sit at home to take physic, and they tell me that I must do nothing that costs me great application or great pains, therefore I can neither say my prayers nor write verses. I am ordered to think but slightly of anything, and I am practising, if I can think so of you, which, if I can bring about, I shall be above regarding anything in nature for the future; I may then think of the world as a hazel nut, the sun as a spangle, and the king's coronation as a puppet show. When my physic makes me remember those I love, may it not be said to work kindly? Hide, I beseech you, this pun from Miss Patty, who hates them in compliance to the taste of a noble earl, whose modesty makes him detest double meanings....

Let me tell her she will never look so finely while she is upon the earth as she would in the water. It is not here, as in most instances, but those ladies that would please extremely must go out of their own element. She does not make half so good a figure on horseback as Christina, Queen of Sweden; but were she once seen in Bath, no man would part with her for the best mermaid in Christendom.

Ladies, I have you so often, I perfectly know how you look in black and white. I have experienced the utmost you can do in any colours; but all your movements, all your graceful steps, all your attitudes and postures, deserve not half the glory you might here attain of a moving and easy behaviour in buckram; something betwixt swimming and walking; free enough, yet more modestly half-naked than you appear anywhere elsewhere.

You have conquered enough already by land; show your ambition, and vanquish also by water. We have no pretty admirers on these seas, but must strike sail to your white flags were they once hoisted up. The buckram I mention is a dress particularly useful at this time, when the Princess is bringing over the fashion of German ruffs. You ought to dress yourself to some degree of stiffness beforehand; and when our ladies' chins have been tickled awhile with a starched muslin and wires, they may possibly bear the brush of a German beard and whisker.

You are to understand, madam, that my *violent* passion for your fair self and your sister has been divided, and with the most wonderful regularity in the world. Even from my infancy, I have been in love with one after the other of you week by week, and my journey to Bath fell out in the three hundred seventh-sixth week of the reign of my sovereign lady Martha. At the present writing hereof it is the three hundred and eighty-ninth week of the reign of your most serene majesty, in whose service I was listed some weeks before I beheld her. This information will account for my writing to either of you hereafter, as she shall happen to be queen regent at that time.

I could tell you a most delightful story of Dr Parnelle, but want room to display it in all its shining circumstances. He had heard it was an excellent cure for love, to kiss the aunt of the person beloved, who is generally of years and experience enough to damp the fiercest flame. He tried this course in his passion for you, and kissed Mrs Englefield at Mrs Dancaster's [Duncastle]. This recipe he hath left written in the style of a divine as follows:–

'Whoso loveth Miss Blount shall kiss her aunt and be healed; for he kisseth her not as her husband, who kisseth and is enslaved for ever as one of the foolish ones; but as a passenger who passeth away and forgetteth the kiss of her mouth, even as the wind saluteth a flower in his passage, and knoweth not the odour thereof.'

George Farquhar to Anne Oldfield
Monday, twelve o'clock at night [1699?]

Give me leave to call you dear madam, and tell you that I am now stepping into bed, and that I speak with as much sincerity as if I were stepping into my grave. Sleep is so great an emblem of death that my words ought to be as real as if I were sure never to awaken; then may I never again be blest with the light of the sun and the joys of *Wednesday* if you are not as dear to me as my hopes of waking in health to-morrow morning. Your charms lead me, my inclinations prompt me, and my reason confirms me. – Madam, your faithful and humble servant.

My humble service to the lady who must be the chief mediator for my happiness.

George Farquhar to Anne Oldfield
Friday night, eleven o'clock [1699?]

If you find no more rest from your thoughts in bed than I do, I could wish you, madam, to be always there, for there I am most in love. I went to the play this evening and the music roused my soul to such a pitch of passion that I was almost mad with melancholy. I flew thence to *Spring Garden* where with envious eyes I saw every man pick up his mate, whilst I alone walked like solitary *Adam* before the creation of *Eve*, but the place was no paradise to me, nothing I found entertaining but the nightingale which methought in sweet notes like your own pronounced the name of my dear *Penelope – as the fool thinketh the bell clinketh*. From hence I retired to the tavern where methought the shining glass represented your fair person, and the sparkling wine within it looked like your lovely wit and spirit. I met my dear mistress in everything, and I propose presently to see her in a lively dream, since the last thing I do is to kiss

her dear letter, clasp her charming ideal in my arms, and
so fall asleep –

> My morning songs, my evening prayers,
> My daily musings, nightly cares.

Adieu!

John Ruskin to Effie Gray   *Folkestone, 30 November 1847*

My Beloved Effie,

I never thought to have felt time pass slowly any
more – but – foolish that I am, I cannot help congratu-
lating myself on this being the last day of November –
Foolish, I say – for what pleasure soever may be in store
for us, we ought not to wish to lose the treasure of time
– nor to squander away the heap of gold even though its
height should keep us from seeing each other for a little
while. But your letter of last night shook all the
philosopher out of me. That little undress bit! Ah – my
sweet Lady – What naughty thoughts had I. Dare I say?
– I was thinking – thinking, naughty – happy thought,
that you would soon have – some one's arms to keep you
from being cold! Pray don't be angry with me. How
could I help it? – how can I? I'm thinking so just now,
even. Oh – my dearest – I am not so 'scornful' neither, of
all that I hope for – Alas – I know not what I would not

give for one glance of your fair eyes – your fair – saucy eyes. You cruel, cruel girl – now that was *just* like you – to poor William at the Ball. I can see you at this moment – *hear* you. '*If* you wanted to dance with *me*, William! *If*!' You saucy – wicked – witching – malicious – merciless – mischief loving – torturing – martyrizing – unspeakably to be feared and fled – mountain nymph that you are – 'If!' When you knew that he would have given a year of his life for a touch of your hand. Ah's me – what a world this is, when its best creatures and kindest – will do such things. What a sad world. Poor fellow, – How the lights of the ballroom would darken and its floor sink beneath him – Earthquake and eclipse at once, and to be 'if'd' at by you, too; Now – I'll take up his injured cause – I'll punish you for that – Effie – some time – see if I don't – *If* I don't. It deserves – oh – I don't know what it doesn't deserve – nor what I can do.

P.S. Ah – my mysterious girl – I forgot one little bit of the letter – but I can't forget *all*, though 'a great many things'.

My heart is yours – my thoughts – myself – all but my memory, but that's mine. Now it is cool – as you say – to give me all that pain – and then tell me – 'Never mind, I won't do it again.' Heaven forbid! How could you – puss? You are not thinking of saying that you have 'been thinking about it –' or 'writing to a friend' – and that you won't have me now! Are you?

'Lewis Carroll' to Gertrude
Christ Church, Oxford, 28 October 1876

My Dearest Gertrude:

You will be sorry, and surprised, and puzzled, to hear what a queer illness I have had ever since you went. I sent for the doctor, and said, 'Give me some medicine, for I'm tired.' He said, 'Nonsense and stuff! You don't want medicine: go to bed!' I said, 'No; it isn't the sort of tiredness that wants bed. I'm tired in the *face*.' He looked a little grave, and said, 'Oh, it's your *nose* that's tired: a person often talks too much when he thinks he nose a great deal.' I said, 'No, it isn't the nose. Perhaps it's the *hair*.' Then he looked rather grave, and said, '*Now* I understand: you've been playing too many hairs on the pianoforte.' 'No, indeed I haven't!' I said, 'and it isn't exactly the *hair*: it's more about the nose and chin.' Then he looked a good deal graver, and said, 'Have you been walking much on your chin lately?' I said, 'No.' 'Well!' he said, 'it puzzles me very much. Do you think that it's in the lips?' 'Of course!' I said. 'That's exactly what it is!'

Then he looked very grave indeed, and said, 'I think you must have been giving too many kisses.' 'Well,' I said, 'I did give one kiss to a baby child, a little friend of mine.' 'Think again,' he said; 'are you sure it was only one?' I thought again, and said, 'Perhaps it was eleven times.' Then the doctor said, 'You must not give her any more till your lips are quite rested again.' 'But what am I to do?' I said, 'because you see, I owe her a hundred and eighty-two more.' Then he looked so grave that the tears ran down his cheeks, and he said, 'You may send them to her in a box.' Then I remembered a little box that I once bought at Dover, and thought I would some day give it to *some* little girl or other. So I have packed them all in it very carefully. Tell me if they come safe or if any are lost on the way.

'Lewis Carroll' to May Mileham   *6 September 1885*

7 Lushington Road, Eastbourne

Dearest May,

Thank you very much indeed for the peaches. They were delicious. Eating one was almost as nice as kissing you: of course not quite: I think, if I had to give the exact measurement, I should say 'three-quarters as nice'. We are having such a lovely time here; and the sands are beautiful. I only wish I could some day come across you, washing your pocket-handkerchief in a pool among the rocks! But I wander on the beach, and look for you, in vain: and then I say, 'Where is May?' And the stupid boatmen reply, 'It isn't May, sir! It's September!' But it doesn't comfort me.

Always your loving

C.L.D.

Stella Campbell to Bernard Shaw   29 July 1912

33 Kensington Square, W

– My Stella used to sing a song which I told her was silly, and she declared was funny – your last letter reminds me more of it than your others –

> He's mad, mad, mad,
> He's clean gone off his nut
> He cleans his boots with strawberry jam
> He eats his hat whenever he can
> He's mad, mad, mad –

– I hope you too will have a lovely holiday and not need your 'cap and bells' all the time – and that bladder-whacking of yours, that makes my dear friend D.D. jump, and imagine its really a bump!

My address will be

Hotel Mirabeau
Aix-les-Bains
Savoie
France –

I start to-morrow after 8 days in bed – with two black eyes – and some screw-like pains in my shoulder.

Yours affectionately,

Beatrice Stella

Lord Byron to Lady Caroline Lamb   Sy even, April 1812

I never supposed you artful, we are *all* selfish, nature did that for us, but even when you attempt deceit occasionally, you cannot maintain it, which is all the better, want of success will curb the tendency. – Every word you utter, every line you write proves you to be either *sincere* or a *fool,* now as I know you are not the one I must believe you the other. I never knew a woman with greater or more pleasing talents, *general* as in a woman they should be, something of everything, & too much of nothing, but these are unfortunately coupled with a total want of common conduct. – For instance the *note* to your *page,* do you suppose I delivered it? or did you mean that I should? I did not of course. – Then your heart – my poor Caro, what a little volcano! that pours *lava* through your veins, & yet I cannot wish it a bit colder, to make a *marble slab* of, as you sometimes see (to understand my foolish metaphor) brought in vases tables &c from Vesuvius when hardened after an eruption. – To drop my detestable tropes & figures you know I have always thought you the cleverest most agreeable, absurd, amiable, perplexing, dangerous fascinating little being that lives now or ought to have lived 2000 years ago. – I wont talk to you of beauty, I am no judge, but our *beauties* cease to be so when near you, and therefore you have either some or something better. And now, Caro, this nonsense is the first and last compliment (if it be such) I ever paid you, you have often reproached me as wanting in that respect, but *others* will make up the deficiency ... All that you so often *say*, I *feel*, can more be said or felt? – This same prudence is tiresome enough but one must maintain it, or what can we do to be saved? – Keep to it. –

[written on cover] If you write at all, write as usual – but do as you please, only as I never see you – Basta!

Richard Steele to his wife   Five in the evening, 19 September 1708

Dear Prue,

I send you seven pen'orth of walnuts at five a penny, which is the greatest proof I can give you at present of my being, with my whole heart, yrs.

The little horse comes back with the boy, who returns with him for me on Wednesday evening; in the meantime, I believe, it will be well that he runs in the Park. I am Mrs Binns's servant.

Since I writ this I came to the place where the boy was order'd with the horses; and, not finding him, sent this bearer, lest you should be in fears, the boy not returning.

P.S. There are but 29 walnuts.

INTOXICATION

Richard Steele to Mary Scurlock
Saturday night [30 August 1707]

Dear, Lovely Mrs Scurlock,

I have been in very good company, where your
unknown name, under the character of the woman I
lov'd best, has been often drunk; so that I may say I am
dead drunk for your sake, which is more than 'I dye for
you.'

Richard Steele to Mary Scurlock
St James's Coffee House, 1 September 1707

Madam – It is the hardest thing in the world to be in
love, and yet attend to business. As for me, all who
speak to me do find out, and I must lock myself up, or
other people will do it for me.

A gentleman asked me this morning, 'What news
from Lisbon?' and I answered, 'She is exquisitely
handsome.' Another desired to know 'when I had been
last at Hampton Court?' I replied, 'It will be on Tuesday
come se'nnight.' Pr'ythee allow me at least to kiss your
hand before that day, that my mind may be in some
composure. O love!

> A thousand torments dwell about thee,
> Yet who would live, to live without thee?

Methinks I could write a volume to you; but all the language on earth would fail in saying how much, and with what disinterested passion, I am ever yours.

My darling,

I am sorry I was late to-day. I had no business to be late. You know I like to be on time. I met Nat Gubbins in a pub and we got talking. I had three sherries only. You ticked me off and I said unkind things to you. I provoked you and went on provoking and could not stop myself. You looked so beautiful. It pleased me to make you cry.

I went away from you. I have had three more sherries. I vowed I would never see you again, but I cannot keep my vow.

Albeit I come back to my love for you.

Caradoc

What am I doing? Heavens, I'm spinning. And I use this verb as a planet would. Yes, I'm spinning. I've seen roses, honeysuckle, forty degrees Centigrade of dazzling heat, moonlight, ancient wisteria enlacing the door of my old home in Saint-Sauveur. I've seen the night over Fontainebleau. And as I said, I'm spinning. Beside me there is a dark boy at the wheel. I'm on my way back to Paris, but shall I stay there? The dark boy beside me is still at the wheel, and how strange everything is! And how good I am, and how amazed I am, and what wise improvidence in my behaviour! Oh yes, I'm spinning!

As you can see, you must not worry about me. From time to time I am uneasy about myself, and I give a start, prick up my ears, and cry out, 'But what are you doing?' and then I refuse to think any more about it . . .

Just now, on the telephone, an enlightened Chiwawa, enlightened by the dark, dark, dark boy, sang my praises. The era of frankness is back and the cards are on the table. But, my Marguerite, how strange it all is! . . . I have the fleeting confidence of people who fall out of a clock tower and for a moment sail through the air in a comfortable fairy-world, feeling no pain anywhere . . .

Franz Kafka to Felice Bauer
Night of 15–16 December 1912

Well dearest, the doors are shut, all is quiet, I am with you once more. How many things does 'to be with you' mean by now? I have not slept all day, and while I duly went about all the afternoon and early evening with a heavy head and a befogged brain, now, as night sets in, I am almost excited, feel within me a tremendous desire to write; the demon inhabiting the writing urge begins to stir at most inopportune moments. Let him, I'll go to bed. But if I could spend Christmas writing and sleeping, dearest, that would be wonderful!

I was after you continuously this afternoon, in vain of course. As a matter of fact not quite in vain, for I constantly kept as close as possible to Frau Friedmann, because after all she was close to you for quite a time, because you say *Du* to each other, and because she happens to be the possessor of letters from you, which I certainly begrudge her. But why doesn't she say a word about you while I keep staring at her lips, ready to pounce on the first word? Have you stopped writing to each other? Perhaps she knows nothing new about you? But how is this possible! And if she knows nothing new, why doesn't she talk about something old? And if she doesn't want to talk about you, why doesn't she at least mention your name, as she used to, when she was around before? But no, she won't; instead, she keeps me hanging about, and we talk about incredibly un-important things, such as Breslau, coughing, music, scarves, brooches, hairstyles, Italian holidays, sleigh-rides, beaded bags, stiff shirts, cufflinks, Herbert Schott-länder, the French language, public baths, showers, cooks, Harden, economic conditions, travelling by night, the Palace Hotel, Schreiberhau, hats, the University of Breslau, relatives – in short about everything under the sun, but the only subject that has, unfortunately, some faint association with you consists of a few words about Pyramidos and aspirin; it is cause for wonder why I pursue this subject for so long, and why I enjoy rolling these two words around my tongue. But really, I am not satisfied with this as the sole outcome of an afternoon, because for hours on end my head hums with the desire to hear the name Felice. Finally, by force, I direct the conversation to the railway connections between Berlin and Breslau, at the same time giving her a menacing look – nothing.

Franz

Alexander Pope to Martha Blount   [*no date*]

Most Divine

– It is some proof of my sincerity towards you, that I write when I am prepared by drinking to speak truth; and sure a letter after twelve at night must abound with that noble ingredient. That heart must have abundance of flames, which is at once warmed by wine and you: wine awakens and expresses the lurking passions of the mind, as varnish does the colours that are sunk in a picture, and brings them out in all their natural glowings. My good qualities have been so frozen and locked up in a dull constitution at all my former sober hours, that it is very astonishing to me, now I am drunk, to find so much virtue in me.

John Keats to Fanny Brawne   [*Monday 11 October 1819*]

College Street

My sweet Girl,

I am living to day in yesterday: I was in a complete fa[s]cination all day. I feel myself at your mercy. Write me ever so few lines and tell you (*for* me) you will never for ever be less kind to me than yesterday —. You dazzled me. There is nothing in the world so bright and delicate. When Brown came out with that seemingly true story again[s]t me last night, I felt it would be death to me if you had ever believed it – though against any one else I could muster up my obstinacy. Before I knew Brown could disprove it I was for the moment miserable. When shall we pass a day alone? I have had a thousand kisses, for which with my whole soul I thank love – but if you should deny me the thousand and first – 'twould put me to the proof how great a misery I could live through. If you should ever carry your threat yesterday into execution – believe me 'tis not my pride, my vanity or any petty passion would torment me – really 'twould hurt my heart – I could not bear it. I have seen Mrs Dilke this morning; she says she will come with me any fine day.

Ever yours

John Keats

Ah hertè mine!

Katherine Mansfield to John Middleton Murry
[28 March 1915]

Jack, I shan't hide what I feel today. I woke up with you in my breast and on my lips. Jack, I love you terribly today. The whole world is gone. There is only you. I walk about, dress, eat, write – but all the time I am *breathing* you. Time and again I have been on the point of telegraphing you that I am coming home as soon as Kay sends my money. It is still possible that I shall.

> Jack, Jack, I want to come back,
> And to hear the little ducks go
> Quack! Quack! Quack!

Life is too short for our love even though we stayed together every moment of all the years. I cannot think of you – our life – our darling life – you, my treasure – everything about you.

No, no, no. Take me quickly into your arms. Tig is a tired girl and she is crying. I want you, I want you. Without you life is nothing.

Your woman

Tig

Alban Berg to Helene Nahowski   Thursday – spring 1909

There is a delicate scent in my room. I have before me the second of your lovely veils, and when I press it to my face, I can almost feel the sweet warm breath from your mouth. The violets you picked for me yesterday, which nearly withered in my buttonhole, are now blooming anew, and smell soft and fresh. The cushion on the divan and the chair by the window belong to you, Helene, they have become appendages to your presence. Indeed everything in my room is the same: the mirror in front of which you arranged your hair; the window I have seen you looking through so seriously (even in our gayest moments); the last pale rays of sunlight which make your hair gleam with gold; the glowing fire in the stove; and then the laurel wreath, and the dear little cover on the bedside table – everything, everything is yours.

And that's no wonder seeing that I myself have become so entirely your 'creation'. All my possessions and even thought are somehow a loan or gift from *you*. Dressing in the morning, for instance, when I get an idea for a theme, a mood, or sometimes even a single chord, at best a whole extended melody – then I always feel it has come flying in from you. It's the same with everything: if I read something out of the ordinary, with difficult parts in it, I imagine myself understanding those parts and penetrating its mysteries only through you, Helene. I mean this reading in the widest sense. If I look at nature with the eyes of a sensitive reader, when I hear music or see paintings or – but why go on with a list of all the things which have come to life in me only through you?

Oh, Helene, how can I live without you!

I am completely yours

Napoleon Bonaparte to Josephine Beauharnais
Paris, December 1795

I wake filled with thoughts of you. Your portrait and the intoxicating evening which we spent yesterday have left my senses in turmoil. Sweet, incomparable Josephine, what a strange effect you have on my heart! Are you angry? Do I see you looking sad? Are you worried? ... My soul aches with sorrow, and there can be no rest for your lover; but is there still more in store for me when, yielding to the profound feelings which overwhelm me, I draw from your lips, from your heart a love which consumes me with fire? Ah! it was last night that I fully realized how false an image of you your portrait gives!

You are leaving at noon; I shall see you in three hours.

Until then, mio dolce amor, a thousand kisses; but give me none in return, for they set my blood on fire.

Vita Sackville-West to Virginia Woolf
Milan [posted in Trieste], Thursday, 21 January 1927

... I am reduced to a thing that wants Virginia. I composed a beautiful letter to you in the sleepless nightmare hours of the night, and it has all gone: I just miss you, in a quite simple desperate human way. You, with all your undumb letters, would never write so elementary a phrase as that; perhaps you wouldn't even feel it. And yet I believe you'll be sensible of a little gap.

But you'd clothe it in so exquisite a phrase that it would lose a little of its reality. Whereas with me it is quite stark: I miss you even more than I could have believed; and I was prepared to miss you a good deal. So this letter is just really a squeal of pain. It is incredible how essential to me you have become. I suppose you are accustomed to people saying these things. Damn you, spoilt creature; I shan't make you love me any the more by giving myself away like this – But oh my dear, I can't be clever and stand-offish with you: I love you too much for that. Too truly. You have no idea how stand-offish I can be with people I don't love. I have brought it to a fine art. But you have broken down my defences. And I don't really resent it.

John Keats to Fanny Brawne
[Wednesday, 13 October 1819]

25 College Street

My dearest Girl,

This moment I have set myself to copy some verses out fair. I cannot proceed with any degree of content. I must write you a line or two and see if that will assist in dismissing you from my Mind for ever so short a time.

67

Upon my Soul I can think of nothing else. The time is passed when I had power to advise and warn you against the unpromising morning of my Life. My love has made me selfish. I cannot exist without you. I am forgetful of every thing but seeing you again – my Life seems to stop there – I see no further. You have absorb'd me. I have a sensation at the present moment as though I was dissolving – I should be exquisitely miserable without the hope of soon seeing you. I should be afraid to separate myself far from you. My sweet Fanny, will your heart never change? My love, will it? I have no limit now to my love – You[r] note came in just here – I cannot be happier away from you. 'Tis richer than an Argosy of Pearles. Do not threat me even in jest. I have been astonished that Men could die Martyrs for religion – I have shudder'd at it. I shudder no more – I could be martyr'd for my Religion – Love is my religion – I could die for that. I could die for you. My Creed is Love and you are its only tenet. You have ravish'd me away by a Power I cannot resist; and yet I could resist till I saw you; and even since I have seen you I have endeavoured often 'to reason against the reasons of my Love'. I can do that no more – the pain would be too great. My love is selfish. I cannot breathe without you.

Yours for ever

John Keats

John Keats to Fanny Brawne
Tuesday morn [19 October 1819]

Great Smith Street

My sweet Fanny,

On awakening from my three days dream ('I cry to dream again') I find one and another astonish'd at my idleness and thoughtlessness. I was miserable last night – the morning is always restorative. I must be busy, or try to be so. I have several things to speak to you of tomorrow morning. Mrs Dilke I should think will tell you that I purpose living at Hampstead. I must impose chains upon myself. I shall be able to do nothing. I sho[u]ld like to cast the die for Love or death. I have no Patience with any thing else – if you ever intend to be cruel to me as you say in jest now but perhaps may sometimes be in earnest be so now – and I will – my mind is in a tremble, I cannot tell what I am writing.

Ever my love yours

John Keats

William Congreve to Arabella Hunt   [*1690?*]

Dear Madam,

Not believe that I love you? You cannot pretend to be so incredulous. If you do not believe my tongue, consult my eyes, consult your own. You will find by yours that they have charms; by mine that I have a heart which feels them. Recall to mind what happened last night. That at least was a lover's kiss. Its eagerness, its fierceness, its warmth, expressed the God its parent. But oh! its sweetness, and its melting softness expressed him more. With trembling in my limbs, and fevers in my soul I ravish'd it. Convulsions, pantings, murmurings shew'd the mighty disorder within me: the mighty disorder increased by it. For those dear lips shot through my heart, and thro' my bleeding vitals, delicious poison, and an avoidless but yet a charming ruin.

What cannot a day produce? The night before I thought myself a happy man, in want of nothing, and in fairest expectation of fortune; approved of by men of wit, and applauded by others. Pleased, nay charmed with my friends, my then dearest friends, sensible of every delicate pleasure, and in their turns possessing all.

But Love, almighty Love, seems in a moment to have removed me to a prodigious distance from every object but you alone. In the midst of crowds I remain in solitude. Nothing but you can lay hold of my mind, and

that can lay hold of nothing but you. I appear trans-
ported to some foreign desert with you (oh, that I were
really thus transported!), where, abundantly supplied
with everything, in thee, I might live out an age of
uninterrupted extasy.

The scene of the world's great stage seems suddenly
and sadly chang'd. Unlovely objects are all around me,
excepting thee; the charms of all the world appear to be
translated to thee. Thus in this said but oh, too pleasing
state! my soul can fix upon nothing but thee; thee it
contemplates, admires, adores, nay depends on, trusts
on you alone.

If you and hope forsake it, despair and endless misery
attend it.

Oscar Wilde to Lord Alfred Douglas   *March 1893*

Savoy Hotel, London

Dearest of all Boys,

Your letter was delightful, red and yellow wine to
me; but I am sad and out of sorts. Bosie, you must not
make scenes with me. They kill me, they wreck the
loveliness of life. I cannot see you, so Greek and
gracious, distorted with passion. I cannot listen to your

curved lips saying hideous things to me. I would sooner be blackmailed by every renter in London than have you bitter, unjust, hating. I must see you soon. You are the divine thing I want, the thing of grace and beauty; but I don't know how to do it. Shall I come to Salisbury? My bill here is £49 for a week. I have also got a new sitting-room over the Thames. Why are you not here, my dear, my wonderful boy? I fear I must leave; no money, no credit, and a heart of lead.

Your own Oscar

Anaïs Nin to Henry Miller   9 March 1932

I can't write to you, Henry, though I was awake last night telling you – all night – of that man I discovered yesterday . . . the man I sensed with my feelings the first moment – all the mountains of words, writings, quotations have sundered – I only know now the splendour, the blinding splendour of your room – and that unreal moment – how can a moment be at once unreal and so warm – so warm.

There is so much you want to know. I remember your phrase: 'Only whores appreciate me'. I wanted to say: you can only have blood-consciousness with whores, there is too much mind between us, too much literature, too much illusion – but then you denied there had been only mind . . .

My face makes you think that all my expectations go up, up . . . but you know now that it is not only my mind which is aware of you.

Aware of you, chaotically. I love this strange, treacherous softness of you which always turns to hatred. How did I single you out? I saw you with that intense selective way – I saw a mouth that was at once intelligent, animal, and soft . . . strange mixture – a human man, sensitively aware of everything – I love awareness – a man, I told you, whom life made drunk. Your laughter was not a laughter which could hurt, it was mellow and rich. I felt warm, dizzy, and I sang within myself. You always said the truest and deepest things – slowly – and you have a way of saying, like a southerner – hem, hem – trailingly, while off on your own introspective journey – which touched me.

Just before that I had sought, as I told you, suicide. But I waited to meet you, as if that would solve something – and it did. When I saw you I thought, here is a man I could love. And I was no longer afraid of feelings. I couldn't go through with the suicide (idea of killing off romanticism), something held me back. I can only move wholly . . .

I don't know if it was love – there was a long moment of interruption – the love for June. Henry – the love for

June is still there. I couldn't bear seeing her [photograph] yesterday. She possesses us both — everything else is only a temporary victory.

I thought I was in love with your mind and genius (I read you what I thought of your mind and writing) chaos only with June. I felt your mind watching me. I didn't want love because it is chaos, and it makes the mind vacillate like wind-blown lanterns. I wanted to be very strong before you, to be *against* you — you love so to be against things. I love to be *for* things. You make caricatures. It takes great hate to make caricatures. I elect, I love — the welling of love stifles me at night — as in that dream which you struggled to make *real* yesterday — to nail down, yes, with your engulfing kiss.

When you will feel me veiled, holding back, Henry, it is June. What power you had that first day, tearing from me pages from my journal about her. You do not know to what extent I guard myself, and my feelings. It is strange how you get truth from me.

ADORATION

John Keats to Fanny Brawne 　[*March 1820?*]

Sweetest Fanny,

　You fear, sometimes, I do not love you so much as you wish? My dear Girl I love you ever and ever and without reserve. The more I have known you the more have I lov'd. In every way – even my jealousies have been agonies of Love, in the hottest fit I ever had I would have died for you. I have vex'd you too much. But for Love! Can I help it? You are always new. The last of your kisses was ever the sweetest; the last smile the brightest; the last movement the gracefullest. When you pass'd my window home yesterday, I was fill'd with as much admiration as if I had then seen you for the first time. You uttered a half complaint once that I only lov'd your Beauty. Have I nothing else then to love in you but that? Do not I see a heart naturally furnish'd with wings imprison itself with me? No ill prospect has been able to turn your thoughts a moment from me. This perhaps should be as much a subject of sorrow as joy – but I will not talk of that. Even if you did not love me I could not help an entire devotion to you: how much more deeply then must I feel for you knowing you love me. My Mind has been the most discontented and restless one that ever was put into a body too small for it. I never felt my Mind repose upon anything with complete and undistracted enjoyment – upon no person but you. When you are in the room my thoughts never fly out of window: you always concentrate my whole senses. The anxiety shown about our Loves in your last note is an immense pleasure to me: however you must not suffer such speculations to molest you any more: nor will I any more believe you can have the least pique against me. Brown is gone out – but here is Mrs Wylie – when she is gone I shall be awake for you. – Remembrances to your Mother.

Your affectionate

J. Keats

Katherine Mansfield to John Middleton Murry
Sunday night [27 January 1918]

My love and my darling,

It is ten minutes past eight. I must tell you how much I love you at ten minutes past eight on a Sunday evening, January 27th 1918.

I have been indoors all day (except for posting your letter) and I feel greatly rested. Juliette has come back from a new excursion into the country, with blue irises – do you remember how beautifully they grew in that little house with the trellis tower round by the rocks? – and all sorts and kinds of sweet-smelling jonquils ... The room is very warm. I have a handful of fire, and the few little flames dance on the log and can't make up their minds to attack it ... There goes a train. Now it is quiet again except for my watch. I look at the minute hand and think what a spectacle I shall make of myself when I am really coming home to you. How I shall sit in the railway carriage, and put the old watch in my lap and pretend to cover it with a book – but not read or see, but just whip it up with my longing gaze, and simply make it go faster.

My love for you tonight is so deep and tender that it seems to be outside myself as well. I am fast shut up like a little lake in the embrace of some big mountains, you would see me down below, deep and shining – and quite fathomless, my dear. You might drop your heart into me and you'd never hear it touch bottom. I love you – I love you – Goodnight.

Oh, Bogey, what it is to love like this!

Bernard Shaw to Stella Campbell
Ayot St Lawrence, Welwyn, 6 February 1913

Stella, Stella what is there left to say?

I have just played all sorts of things, almost accurately, I dont believe I could get a headache if I tried. I drove from Hatfield faster than a man should drive in the dark.

What an enormous meal of happiness! They will wish you many happy returns of Sunday. Sunday! I laugh hollowly. When I am dead let them put an inscription on 12 Hinde St HERE A GREAT MAN FOUND HAPPINESS. Wagner wrote up on his house Hier wo mein Wahnen Frieden fand (Wahnfried sei dieses Haus genannt) (if I recollect it aright). Nobody can translate it; but I understand it. I will write on the sky someday.

I was only twenty minutes late for my appointment; and if I had been wise enough to miss it altogether I should have saved £300; for that is just what keeping it cost me in money. What it cost me in absence three hundred millions could not pay for.

Her last words as we parted (very affectionately on my part) were 'I never know where you spend your afternoons. Once I never thought about it – never doubted. Now – I always imagine –' I see you, like the Flying Dutchman, once in seven years; and I am supposed to see you every seven minutes. It is amazing to myself that I dont. How is it that I will get up and trudge through the mud to any sort of miserable work, but that I must always let heaven come to me? I should not have come up today but for that silly committee and two other utterly frivolous businesses. It is incredible. How did I get it ground into me that happiness is always picked up on the way and must not be sought? Yet there is something in it: it came nobly off today. Stella: I *WAS* happy. Was! I *am*. I shall never be unhappy again.

You cannot have this in the morning because the evening post, at six, had gone before I returned; so this must wait until morning (12) and will reach you in the afternoon – oh Stella Stella Stella Stella Stella Stella

G.B.S.

Zelda Fitzgerald to F. Scott Fitzgerald [1920]

I look down the tracks and see you coming – and out of every haze & mist your darling rumpled trousers are hurrying to me – Without you, dearest dearest I couldn't see or hear or feel or think – or live – I love you so and I'm never in all our lives going to let us be apart another night. It's like begging for mercy of a storm or killing Beauty or growing old, without you. I want to kiss you so – and in the back where your dear hair starts and your chest – I love you – and I can't tell you how much – To think that I'll *die* without your knowing – Goofo, you've *got* to try [to] feel how much I do – how inanimate I am when you're gone – I can't even hate

81

these damnable people – Nobodys got any right to live but us – and they're dirtying up our world and I can't hate them because I want you so – Come Quick – Come Quick to me – I could never do without you if you hated me and were covered with sores like a leper – if you ran away with another woman and starved me and beat me – I still would want you *I know* –

Lover, Lover, Darling –

Your Wife

Napoleon Bonaparte to Josephine Bonaparte
Nice, 10 Germinal, year IV [1796]

To citizen Bonaparte,
care of citizen Beauharnais,
6, rue Chantereine, Paris.

I have not spent a day without loving you; I have not spent a night without embracing you; I have not so much as drunk one cup of tea without cursing the pride and ambition which force me to remain apart from the moving spirit of my life. In the midst of my duties, whether I am at the head of my army or inspecting the camps, my beloved Josephine stands alone in my heart, occupies my mind, fills my thoughts. If I am moving away from you with the speed of the Rhône torrent, it is only that I may see you again more quickly. If I rise to work in the middle of the night, it is because this may hasten by a matter of days the arrival of my sweet love. Yet in your letter of the 23rd and 26th Ventôse, you call me *vous*. *Vous* yourself! Ah! wretch, how could you have written this letter? How cold it is! And then there are those four days between the 23rd and the 26th; what were you doing that you failed to write to your husband? ... Ah, my love, that *vous*, those four days make me long for my former indifference. Woe to the person responsible! May he, as punishment and penalty, experience what my convictions and the evidence (which is in your friend's favour) would make me experience! Hell has no torments great enough! Nor do the Furies have serpents enough! *Vous! Vous!* Ah! how will things stand in two weeks? ... My spirit is heavy; my heart is fettered and I am terrified by my fantasies ... You love me less; but you will get over the loss. One day you will love me no longer; at least tell me; then I shall know how I have come to deserve this misfortune ... Farewell, my wife: the torment, joy, hope and moving spirit of my life; whom I love, whom I fear, who fills me with tender feelings which draw me close to Nature, and with violent impulses as tumultuous as thunder. I ask of you neither eternal love, nor fidelity, but simply ... *truth*, unlimited honesty. The day when you say 'I love you less', will mark the end of my love and the last day of my life. If my heart were base enough to love without being loved in return I would tear it to pieces. Josephine! Josephine! Remember what I have sometimes said to you: Nature has endowed me with a virile and decisive character. It has built yours out of lace and gossamer. Have you ceased to love me? Forgive me, love of my life, my soul is racked by conflicting forces.

My heart, obsessed by you, is full of fears which prostrate me with misery ... I am distressed not to be calling you by name. I shall wait for you to write it.

Farewell! Ah! if you love me less you can never have loved me. In that case I shall truly be pitiable.

Bonaparte

P.S. – The war this year has changed beyond recognition. I have had meat, bread and fodder distributed; my armed cavalry will soon be on the march. My soldiers are showing inexpressible confidence in me; you alone are a source of chagrin to me; you alone are the joy and torment of my life. I send a kiss to your children, whom you do not mention. By God! If you did, your letters would be half as long again. Then visitors at ten o'clock in the morning would not have the pleasure of seeing you. Woman!!!

John Ruskin to Lady Mount-Temple   4 October 1872

My dearest Isola,

The good that you may be sure you have done me remember, is in my having known, actually, for one whole day, the *perfect* joy of love. For I think, to be *quite* perfect, it must still have *some* doubt and pain – the pride of war and patience added to the intense actual pleasure. I don't think any *quite* accepted & beloved lover could have the Kingly and Servantly joy together, as I had it in that ferry boat of yours, when she went into it herself, and stood at the stern, and let me stop it in mid-stream and look her full in the face for a long minute, before she said 'Now go on' – The beautiful place – the entire peace – nothing but birds & squirrels near – the trust, which I had then in all things being – finally well – yet the noble fear mixed with the enchantment – her remaining still above me, not mine, and yet mine.

And this after ten years of various pain – and thirst. And this with such a creature to love – For you know, Isola, people may think her pretty or not pretty – as their taste may be, but she is a *rare* creature, and that kind of beauty happening to be *exactly* the kind I like, – and my whole life being a worship of beauty, – fancy how it intensifies the whole.

Of course, every lover, good for anything, thinks his mistress perfection – but what a difference between this instinctive, foolish – groundless preference, and my deliberate admiration of R, as I admire a thin figure in a Perugino fresco, saying 'it is the loveliest figure I know after my thirty years study of art' – Well – suppose the Perugino – better than Pygmalions statue, – holier – longer sought, *had* left the canvas – come into the garden – walked down to the riverside with me – looked happy – been happy, (– for she *was* – and said she was) – in being with me.

Was'nt it a day, to have got for me? – all your getting.

And clear gain – I am no worse now than I was, – a day or two more of torment and disappointment are as nothing in the continued darkness of my life. But that day is worth being born and living seventy years of pain for.

And I can still read my Chaucer, and write before-breakfast letters – Mad, or dead, she is still mine, now.

Emily Dickinson to Susan Gilbert (Dickinson)
about 6 February 1852

Will you let me come dear Susie – looking just as I do, my dress soiled and worn, my grand old apron, and my hair – Oh Susie, time would fail me to enumerate my appearance, yet I love you just as dearly as if I was e'er so fine, so you wont care, will you? I am so glad dear Susie – that our hearts are always clean, and always neat and lovely, so not to be ashamed. I have been hard at work this morning, and I ought to be working now – but I cannot deny myself the luxury of a minute or two with you.

The dishes may wait dear Susie – and the uncleared table stand, *them* I have always with me, but you, I have 'not always' – *why* Susie, Christ hath saints *manie* – and I have *few*, but thee – the angels shant have Susie – no – no no!

Vinnie is sewing away like a *fictitious* seamstress, and I half expect some knight will arrive at the door, confess himself a *nothing* in presence of her loveliness, and present his heart and hand as the only vestige of him worthy to be refused.

Vinnie and I have been talking about growing old, today. Vinnie thinks *twenty* must be a fearful position for one to occupy – I tell her I dont care if I am young or not, had as lief be thirty, and you, as most anything else. Vinnie expresses her sympathy at my 'sere and yellow leaf' and resumes her work, dear Susie, tell me how *you* feel – ar'nt there days in one's life when to be old dont seem a thing so sad –

I do feel gray and grim, this morning, and I feel it would be a comfort to have a piping voice, and broken back, and scare little children. Dont *you* run, Susie dear, for I wont do any harm, and I do love you dearly tho' I do feel so frightful.

Oh my darling one, how long you wander from me, how weary I grow of waiting and looking, and calling for you; sometimes I shut my eyes, and shut my heart towards you, and try hard to forget you because you grieve me so, but you'll never go away, Oh you never will – say, Susie, promise me again, and I will smile faintly – and take up my little cross again of sad – *sad* separation. How vain it seems to *write*, when one knows how to feel – how much more near and dear to sit beside you, talk with you, hear the tones of your voice; so hard to 'deny thyself, and take up thy cross, and follow me' – give me strength, Susie, write me of hope and love, and of hearts that *endured*, and great was their reward of 'Our Father who art in Heaven.' I dont know how I shall bear it, when the gentle spring comes; if she should come and see me and talk to me of you, Oh it would surely kill me! While the frost clings to the windows, and the World is stern and drear; this absence is easier; the *Earth* mourns too, for all her little birds; but when they all come back again, and she sings and is so merry – pray what will become of me? Susie, forgive me, forget all what I say, get some sweet little scholar to read a gentle hymn, about Bethleem and Mary, and you will sleep on sweetly and have as peaceful dreams, as if I had never written you all these ugly things. Never mind the letter Susie, I wont be angry with you if you dont give me any at all – for I know how busy you are, and how little of that dear strength remains when it is evening, with which to think and write. Only *want* to write me, only sometimes sigh that you are far from me, and that will do, Susie! Dont you think we are good and patient, to let you go so long; and dont we think you're a darling, a real beautiful hero, to toil for people, and teach them, and leave your own dear home? Because we pine and repine, dont think we forget the precious patriot at war in other lands! Never be mournful, Susie – be happy and have cheer, for how many of the long days have gone away since I wrote you – and it is almost noon, and soon the night will come, and then there is one less day of the long pilgrimage. Mattie is very smart, talks of you *much*, my darling; I must leave you now – 'one little hour of Heaven,' thank who did give it me, and will he also grant me one longer and *more* when it shall please his love – bring Susie home, ie! Love always, and ever, and true!

Emily

Oscar Wilde to Lord Alfred Douglas   [*c. 1891*]

My own dear boy – Your sonnet is quite lovely and it is a marvel that those red roseleaf lips of yours should be made no less for the music of song than for the madness of kissing. Your slim gilt soul walks between passion and poetry. I know that Hyacinthus, whom Apollo loved so madly, was you in Greek days. Why are you alone in London, and when do you go to Salisbury? Do go there and cool your hands in the grey twilight of Gothic things, and come here whenever you like. It is a lovely place; it only lacks you, but go to Salisbury first. Always with undying love,

Yours,

Oscar

Bernard Shaw to Stella Campbell   14 February 1913

10 Adelphi Terrace, WC

Stella: I must break myself of this: there is some natural magic in it, some predestined adorability for me in you, that makes me quite reckless when I am within reach of you. It is the dark lady the child dreamt of.

Tomorrow is cram-full – full I tell you: I have not a moment between lunch and my train. And yet I know that I *can* break through and snatch a moment between 4.30 and 5.45, which is the very last second.

Oh what a will-less creature I am! I have taken my farewell, gone back for my last appearance, returned for my positively last appearance, and am madly going again tomorrow for my last appearance but 500,000,000,000,000,000,000,000,000,000,000.

Something was worrying you – but what is that to me? Once I was capable of being helpful – even wanted to be helpful. Now I am a mere predatory creature seeking my prey, my mysteriously natural prey. A parasite. I! *I!!!* It is worse than the tide that I turned to swim against and after five strokes found myself ten yards farther out. Only then I tried but couldnt. Now I could but wont try. That is the dangerous symptom. For I tell you I could. I feel in me the strength to do things a hundred times harder. And I *wont* – yet. Not until the very last moment.

I have never missed the train yet – nor saved it by more than a few seconds. If I ever lose it I shall never come again; for then I shall know that I am not strong enough to save either you or myself, and must fly. So oh Stella, dont ever let me lose it. Dont let me hurt anyone to whom I am bound by all the bonds except the bond of the child to the dark lady. For then I should know myself to be an utter brute and my halo would go out like an extinguished candle. Oh this loathsome but necessary conscience! And oh! this wild happiness that frees me from it!

I saw you first in a dream 43 years ago. I have only just remembered it.

G.B.S.

Honoré de Balzac to Madame Hanska
Friday [12 December 1845]

For me, my dearest love, there are twenty-three sacred towns. They are these: Neuchâtel, Geneva, Vienna, St Petersburg, Dresden, Cannstadt, Karlsruhe, Strasbourg, Passy, Fontainebleau, Orléans, Bourges, Tours, Blois, Paris, Rotterdam, the Hague, Antwerp, Brussels, Baden, Lyon, Toulon, Naples. I do not know what they mean to you but for me, when I think of one of these names, it is as if a Chopin were touching a piano key; the hammer awakens sounds which reverberate through my soul, and a whole poem takes shape.

Neuchâtel is like a white lily, pure, filled with pervasive scents; youth, freshness, excitement, hope, fleetingly perceived happiness. Geneva is the passion of dreams, the kind of dream where life is flashed before one, offered for ... oh! my God, I would have died of ecstasy had I been able to kiss your hand! And what an evening! What youth! I cannot think how you could fail to keep that sodden piece of silk as I have kept the cloth with which I brushed away the fluff from a certain place on the floor which will be before my eyes when I die! ... Geneva is our zenith; our golden harvest! Vienna is mourning in the midst of joy. I came, certain of having nothing but sadness before me; Vienna, my purest act of devotion. And St Petersburg? The blue salon of la Néva!

the first initiation of my sweetheart, the first step in her
education. What a union: it lasted for two months
without a false note, unless one is to count that
argument over the hat and the one about the expense of
engaging a cook. The first moments of our free
encounter; the dawn of the marriage of our souls and the
apprehensions of my precious pet fill these memories
with delight, for I know that she will return to them to
find reasons for loving more strongly, when she sees
how unfair to her poor Noré her misconceptions were.
Dresden is hunger and thirst, misery in the midst of
happiness, a poor man casting himself on the richest of
all feasts. Karlsruhe, the alms given to a pauper. But
Strasbourg, oh! we are sure of love by now, it has the
splendour of Louis XIV; it holds the certain promise of
mutual happiness. And Passy, Fontainebleau? Here is
the genius of Beethoven; the sublime! Orléans, Bourges,
Tours and Blois are concertos, well-loved symphonies,
each of a more or less sunny character but tinged with
sombre notes from my sweetheart's suffering. Paris,
Rotterdam, the Hague, Antwerp are the last blooms of
autumn. But Brussels is worthy of Cannstadt and of us.
It is the triumph of two uniquely loving spirits. I think
of it often and I feel us to be inexhaustible. Baden was
the culmination; harmony for all eternity. There was all
the passion of Geneva, of that evening when I saw you
again; and the combined desires of two mutually

adoring hearts. But Lyon! oh! Lyon, showed me my love transcended by a charm, a tenderness, an ideal quality of caresses and a loving gentleness which makes Lyon for me one of those shibboleths special in a man's life, and which, when spoken, are like the holy word with which a man may open the path to heaven! Toulon is the daughter of Lyon, while all these riches were crowned by the delights of Naples, worthy of heaven, nature and these two sweethearts.

Such then are my flights of fancy when, weary of writing, I think of the rare perfection of her who was at birth so aptly named Eve, for she is unique on earth; there cannot be another so angelic, no other woman who could embody more gentleness, more ingenuity, more love, more inspiration in her caresses. Oh! all memories of Madame de B. are distant indeed! True love, the love of a young and beautiful woman, endowed with such charms, has nothing to fear. So, dearest heart, you are loved and your darling little treasure is kissed a hundred times a day in my thoughts. Guard it well. A thousand embraces to remind us of our twenty-three towns.

Gustave Flaubert to Louise Colet
Croisset, midnight, 8–9 August [1846]

My deplorable mania for analysis exhausts me. I doubt everything, even my doubt. You thought me young, and I am old. I have often spoken with old people about the pleasures of this earth, and I have always been astonished by the brightness that comes into their lacklustre eyes; just as they could never get over their amazement at my way of life, and kept saying 'At your age! At your age! You! You!' Take away my nervous exaltation, my fantasy of mind, the emotion of the moment, and I have little left. That's what I am underneath. *I was not made to enjoy life.* You must not take these words in a down-to-earth sense, but rather grasp their metaphysical intensity. I keep telling myself that I'll bring you misfortune, that were it not for me your life would have continued undisturbed, that the day will come when we shall part (and I protest in advance). Then the nausea of life rises to my lips, and I feel immeasurable self-disgust and a wholly Christian tenderness for you.

At other times – yesterday, for example, when I had sealed my letter – the thought of you sings, smiles, shines, and dances like a joyous fire that gives out a thousand colours and penetrating warmth. I keep remembering the graceful, charming, provocative movement of your mouth when you speak – that rosy, moist mouth that calls forth kisses and sucks them irresistibly in. What a good idea I had, to take your slippers. If you knew how I keep looking at them! The bloodstains are fading: is that their fault? We shall do the same: one year, two years, six, what does it matter? Everything measurable passes, everything that can be counted has an end. Only three things are infinite: the sky in its stars, the sea in its drops of water; and the heart in its tears. Only in that capacity is the heart large; everything else about it is small. Am I lying? Think, try to be calm. One or two shreds of happiness fill it to overflowing, whereas it has room for all the miseries of mankind.

By the way – so we'll christen the blue dress together. I'll try to arrive some evening about six. We'll have all night and the next day. We'll set the night ablaze! I'll be your desire, you'll be mine, and we'll gorge ourselves on each other to see whether we can be satiated. Never! No, never! Your heart is an inexhaustible spring, you let me drink deep, it floods me, penetrates me, I drown. Oh! The beauty of your face, all pale and quivering under my kisses! But how cold I was! I did nothing but look at you; I was surprised, charmed. If I had you here now ... Come, I'll take another look at your slippers. They are something I'll never give up; I think I love them as much as I do you. Whoever made them, little suspected how my hands would tremble when I touch them. I breathe their perfume; they smell of verbena – and of you in a way that makes my heart swell.

Adieu, my life, adieu my love, a thousand kisses everywhere. Phidias has only to write, and I will come. Next winter there will no longer be any way for us to see each other, but if Phidias writes between now and the beginning of the winter I'll come to Paris for at least three weeks. Adieu, I kiss you in the place where I *will* kiss you, where I wanted to; I put my mouth there, je me roule sur toi, mille baisers. Oh! donne-m'en, donne-m'en!

Dorothy Osborne to Sir William Temple

Sir,

If you have ever loved me do not refuse the last request I shall ever make you; 'tis to preserve yourself from the violence of your passion. Vent it all upon me; call me and think me what you please; make me, if it be possible, more wretched than I am. I'll bear it all without the least murmur. Nay, I deserve it all, for had you never seen me you had certainly been happy. 'Tis my misfortunes only that have that infectious quality as to strike at the same time me and all that's dear to me. I am the most unfortunate woman breathing, but I was never false. No; I call heaven to witness that if my life could satisfy for the least injury my fortune has done you (I cannot say 'twas I that did them you), I would lay it down with greater joy than any person ever received a crown; and if I ever forgot what I owe you, or ever entertained a thought of kindness for any person in the world besides, may I live a long and miserable life. 'Tis the greatest curse I can invent; if there be a greater, may I feel it. This is all I can say. Tell me if it be possible I can do anything for you, and tell me how I may deserve your pardon for all the trouble I have given you. I would not die without it.

Dorothy Osborne to Sir William Temple

... 'Twill be pleasinger to you, I am sure, to tell how fond I am of your lock. Well, in earnest now, and setting aside all compliments, I never saw finer hair, nor of a better colour; but cut no more on't, I would not have it spoiled for the world. If you love me, be careful on't. I am combing, and curling, and kissing this lock all day, and dreaming on't all night. The ring, too, is very well, only a little of the biggest. Send me a tortoise one that is a little less than that I sent for a pattern. I would not have the rule so absolutely true without exception that hard hairs be ill-natured, for then I should be so. But I can allow that all soft hairs are good, and so are you, or I am deceived as much as you are if you think I do not love you enough. Tell me, my dearest, am I? You will not be if you think I am

Yours.

Robert Browning to Elizabeth Barrett
1 p.m. Saturday [postmark, 12 September 1846]

You will only expect a few words – what will those be? When the heart is full it may run over, but the real fulness stays within.

You asked me yesterday 'if I should repent?' Yes – my own Ba, – I could wish all the past were to do over again, that in it I might somewhat more, – never so little more, conform in the outward homage to the inward feeling. What I have professed ... (for I have performed nothing) seems to fall short of what my first love required even – and when I think of *this* moment's love ... I could repent, as I say.

Words can never tell you, however, – form them, transform them anyway, – how perfectly dear you are to me – perfectly dear to my heart and soul.

I look back, and in every one point, every word and gesture, *every* letter, every silence – you have been entirely perfect to me – I would not change one word, one look.

My hope and aim are to preserve this love, not to fall

from it – for which I trust to God who procured it for me, and doubtlessly can preserve it.

Enough now, my dearest, dearest, own Ba! You have given me the highest, completest proof of love that ever one human being gave another. I am all gratitude – and all pride (under the proper feeling which ascribes pride to the right source) all pride that my life has been so crowned by you.

God bless you prays your very own R.

I will write to-morrow of course. Take every care of *my life* which is in that dearest little hand; try and be composed, my beloved.

Remember to thank Wilson for me.

Elizabeth Barrett Browning to Robert Browning
Sunday [postmark, 14 September 1846]

My Own Beloved, if ever you should have reason to complain of me in things voluntary and possible, all other women would have a right to tread me underfoot, I should be so vile and utterly unworthy. There is my answer to what you wrote yesterday of wishing to be better to me ... you! What could be better than lifting me from the ground and carrying me into life and the sunshine? I was yours rather by right than by gift (yet by gift also, my beloved!); for what you have saved and renewed is surely yours. All that I am, I owe you – if I enjoy anything now and henceforth, it is through you. You know this well. Even as *I*, from the beginning, knew that I had no power against you . . . or that, if I *had* it was for your sake.

Dearest, in the emotion and confusion of yesterday morning, there was yet room in me for one thought which was not a feeling – for I thought that, of the many, many women who have stood where I stood, and to the same end, not one of them all perhaps, not one perhaps, since that building was a church, has had reasons strong as mine, for an absolute trust and devotion towards the man she married, – not one! And then I both thought and felt, that it was only just, for them . . . those women who were less happy . . . to have that affectionate sympathy and support and presence of their nearest relations, parent or sister . . . which failed to *me*, . . . needing it less through being happier!

Dylan Thomas to Pamela Hansford Johnson
Laugharne, 11 May 1934

I am tortured to-day by every doubt and misgiving that an hereditarily twisted imagination, an hereditary thirst and a commercial quenching, a craving for a body not my own, a chequered education and too much egocentric poetry, and a wild, wet day in a tided town, are capable of conjuring up out of their helly deeps.

Helly deeps. There is torture in words, torture in their linking & spelling, in the snail of their course on stolen paper, in their sound that the four winds double, and in my knowledge of their inadequacy. With a priggish weight on the end, the sentence falls. All sentences fall when the weight of the mind is distributed unevenly along the holy consonants & vowels. In the beginning was a word I can't spell, not a reversed Dog, or a physical light, but a word as long as Glastonbury and as short as pith. Nor does it lisp like the last word, break wind like Balzac through a calligraphied window, but speaks out sharp & everlastingly with the intonations of death and doom on the magnificent syllables. I wonder whether I love your word, the word of your hair – by loving hair I reject all Oscardom, for homosexuality is as bald as a coot – the word of your voice. The word of your flesh, & the word of your presence. However good, I can never love you as earth. The good earth of your blood is always there, under the skin I love, but it is two worlds. There must be only half a world tangible, audible, & visible to the illiterate. And is that the better half? Or is it the wholly ghostly past? And does the one-eyed ferryman, who cannot read a printed word, row over a river of words, where the syllables of the fish dart out & are caught on his rhyming hook, or feel himself a total ghost in a world that's as matter-of-fact as a stone?

SEPARATION

Thomas Hood to his wife   [*no date*]

My own dearest and best,

   We parted manfully and womanfully as we ought. I drank only half a bottle of the Rhine wine, and only the half of that, ere I fell asleep on the sofa, which lasted two hours. It was the reaction, for your going tired me more than I cared to show. Then I drank the other half, and as that did not do, I went and retraced our walk in the park, and sat down in *the same seat*, and felt happier and better. Have you not a romantic old husband?

Jane Welsh Carlyle to Thomas Carlyle
St Leonards-on-Sea, 25 April 1864

Oh my Husband! I am suffering torments! each day I suffer more horribly.

   Oh, I would like you beside me! – I am terribly *alone* – But I don't want to interrupt your work. I will wait till we are in our own hired house and then if I am no better you must come for a day.

Your own wretched

JWC

Mary Wollstonecraft to Gilbert Imlay
Paris, evening, 23 September 1794

I have been playing and laughing with the little girl so long, that I cannot take up my pen to address you without emotion. Pressing her to my bosom, she looked so like you (entre nous, your best looks, for I do not admire your commercial face), every nerve seemed to vibrate to the touch, and I began to think that there was something in the assertion of man and wife being one – for you seemed to pervade my whole frame, quickening the beat of my heart, and lending me the sympathetic tears you excited.

Have I anything more to say to you? No; not for the present – the rest is all flown away; and indulging tenderness for you, I cannot now complain of some people here, who have ruffled my temper for two or three days past.

Zelda Sayre to F. Scott Fitzgerald   *[Spring 1919]*

Sweetheart,

Please, please don't be so depressed – We'll be married soon, and then these lonesome nights will be over forever – and until we are, I am loving, loving every tiny minute of the day and night – Maybe you won't understand this, but sometimes when I miss you most, it's hardest to write – and you always know when I make myself – Just the ache of it all – and I *can't* tell you. If we were together, you'd feel how strong it is – you're so sweet when you're melancholy. I love your sad tenderness – when I've hurt you – That's one of the reasons I could never be sorry for our quarrels – and they bothered you so – Those dear, dear little fusses, when I always tried so hard to make you kiss and forget –

Scott – there's nothing in all the world I want but you – and your precious love – All the material things are nothing. I'd just hate to live a sordid, colorless existence – because you'd soon love me less – and less – and I'd do anything – anything – to keep your heart for my own – I don't want to live – I want to love first, and live incidentally – Why don't you feel that I'm waiting – I'll come to you, Lover, when you're ready – Don't – don't ever think of the things you can't give me – You've trusted me with the dearest heart of all – and it's so damn much more than anybody else in all the world has ever had –

How can you think deliberately of life without me – If you should die – O Darling – darling Scott – It'd be like going blind. I know I would, too, – I'd have no purpose in life – just a pretty – decoration. Don't you think I was made for you? I feel like you had me ordered – and I was delivered to you – to be worn – I want you to wear me, like a watch-charm or a button hole boquet – to the world. And then, when we're alone, I want to help – to know that you can't do *anything* without me.

I'm glad you wrote Mamma. It was such a nice sincere letter – and mine to St Paul was very evasive and rambling. I've never, in all my life, been able to say anything to people older than me – Somehow I just instinctively avoid personal things with them – even my family. Kids are so much nicer.

Queen Mary II to King William III
Whitehall, 19/29 June 1690

You will be weary of seeing every day a letter from me, it may be; yet being apt to flatter myself, I will hope you will be as willing to read as I to write. And indeed it is the only comfort I have in this world, besides that of trust in God. I have nothing to say to you at present that is worth writing, and I think it unreasonable to trouble you with my grief, which I must continue while you are absent, though I trust every post to hear some good news or other from you; therefore, I shall make this very short, and only tell you I have got a swell'd face, though not quite so bad yet, as it was in Holland five years ago. I believe it came by standing too much at the window when I took the waters. I cannot enough thank God for your being so well past the dangers of the sea; I beseech him in his mercy still to preserve you so, and send us once more a happy meeting upon earth. I long to hear again from you how the air of Ireland agrees with you, for I must own I am not without fears for that, loving you so entirely as I do, and shall till death.

Alexander Hamilton to his wife   August 1781

In my last letter I informed you that there was a greater prospect of activity now, than there had been hereto-fore. I did this to prepare your mind for an event, which, I am sure, will give you pain. I begged your father at the same time to intimate to you by degrees the probability of its taking place. I used this method to prevent a surprise which might be too severe to you. A part of the army, my dear girl, is going to Virginia, and I must of necessity be separated at a much greater distance from my beloved wife. I cannot announce the fatal necessity without feeling everything that a fond husband can feel. I am unhappy; – I am unhappy beyond expression. I am unhappy because I am to be so remote from you; because I am to hear from you less frequently than I am accustomed to do. I am miserable because I know you will be so; I am wretched at the idea of flying so far from you, without a single hour's interview, to tell you all my pains and all my love. But I cannot ask permission to visit you. It might be thought improper to leave my corps at such a time and upon such an occasion. I must go without seeing you, – I must go without embracing you: – alas! I must go. But let no idea, other than of the distance we shall be asunder, disquiet you. Though I said the prospects of activity will be greater, I said it to give your expectations a different turn, and prepare you for something disagreeable. It is ten to one that our views will be disappointed, by Cornwallis retiring to South Carolina by land. At all events, our operations will be over by the latter end of October, and I will fly to my home. Don't mention I am going to Virginia.

Evelyn Waugh to Laura Herbert
Wednesday night [5 August 1936]

Grand Hotel Subasio, Assisi

My darling,

It is a night of inconceivable beauty – cool after a stifling day. They have put on the lights in the garden for the first time since I've been here and are proud of them. 'The garden' is a little terrace roofed in leaves with a monkey in a cage and two doves in another.

There is an absurd little fountain – a single jet of water three foot high & they have lit that up too so that it looks like a damp firework. From the terrace one can see the lights of Perugia and all the Umbrian plain and, quite near, the cloister of the Franciscans jutting out over the cliff and they are having their hour of recreation & making a noise as if it is an orgy. Am I writing like a guide book? I hope not. It is just that I feel transported with the beauty of the night & wish you were here to share it. Assisi seems to be full of the Grace of God. Darling Laura I do so wish you were here.

I thought it was going to be easy to leave you for a time. Don't get that wrong. What I mean is that I thought it would be easier for me than you, that I should be seeing so many different things & people that I should not be all the time longing for you. Well I was wrong. I need you all the time – when I'm vexed and uncertain & tired – but more than ever on a night like this when everything is unearthly & lovely.

You see, darling child, so often when people fall in love & want to be married, it is because they foresee a particular kind of life to which the other is necessary. But I dont feel that. Sometimes I think it would be lovely to lead the sort of life with you that I have led alone for the last ten years – no possessions, no home, sometimes extravagant & luxurious, sometimes lying low & working hard. At other times I picture a settled patriarchal life with a large household, rather ceremonious & rather frugal, and sometimes a minute house, and few friends, and little work & leisure & love. But what I do know is that I cant picture any sort of life without you. I have left half of myself behind in England and I am only dragging about a bit of myself now.

And I dont at all regret the haphazard, unhappy life I've led up till now because I dont think that without it I could love you so much. Goodnight my blessed child. I love you more than I can find words to tell you.

E

Nathaniel Hawthorne to Sophia Hawthorne
Boston, 17 April 1839

My Dearest,

I feel pretty secure against intruders, for the bad weather will defend me from foreign invasion; and as to Cousin Haley, he and I had a bitter political dispute last evening, at the close of which he went to bed in high dudgeon, and probably will not speak to me these three days. Thus you perceive that strife and wrangling, as well as east-winds and rain, are the methods of a kind Providence to promote my comfort, – which would not have been so well secured in any other way. Six or seven hours of cheerful solitude! But I will not be alone. I invite your spirit to be with me, — at any hour and as many hours as you please, — but especially at the twilight hour, before I light my lamp. I bid you at that particular time, because I can see visions more vividly in the dusky glow of firelight than either by daylight or lamplight. Come, and let me renew my spell against headache and other direful effects of the east-wind. How I wish I could give you a portion of my insensibility! and yet I should be almost afraid of some radical transformation, were I to produce a change in that respect. If you cannot grow plump and rosy and tough and vigorous without being changed into another nature, then I do think, for this short life, you had better remain just what you are. Yes; but you will be the same to me, because we have met in Eternity, and there our intimacy was formed. So get well as soon as you possibly can, and I shall never doubt that you are the same Sophie who have so often leaned upon my arm and needed its superfluous strength. I never, till now, had a friend who could give me repose; all have disturbed me, and, whether for pleasure or pain, it was still disturbance. But peace overflows from your heart into mine. Then I feel that there is a Now, and that Now must be always calm and happy, and that sorrow and evil are but phantoms that seem to flit across it . . .

When this week's first letter came, I held it a long

time in my hand, marvelling at the superscription. How did you contrive to write it? Several times since I have pored over it, to discover how much of yourself mingled with my share of it; and certainly there is grace flung over the fac-simile, which never was seen in my harsh, uncouth autograph, and yet none of the strength is lost. You are wonderful.

What a beautiful day! and I had a double enjoyment of it – for your sake and my own. I have been to walk, this afternoon, to Bunker's Hill and the Navy Yard, and am tired, because I had not your arm to support me.

God keep you from east-winds and every other evil.

Your own friend,

N.H.

Sophia Hawthorne to Nathaniel Hawthorne
31 December 1839

Best Beloved,

I send you some allumettes wherewith to kindle the taper. There are very few but my second finger could no longer perform extra duty. These will serve till the wounded one be healed, however. How beautiful is it to provide even this slightest convenience for you, dearest! I cannot tell you how much I love you, in this backhanded style. My love is not in this attitude, – it rather bends forward to meet you.

What a year has this been to us! My definition of Beauty is, that it is love, and therefore includes both truth and good. But those only who love as we do can feel the significance and force of this.

My ideas will not flow in these crooked strokes. God be with you. I am very well, and have walked far in Danvers this cold morning. I am full of the glory of the day. God bless you this night of the old year. It has proved the year of our nativity. Has not the old earth passed away from us? – are not all things new?

Your Sophie

Eloïse to Abelard   *[Early 12th century]*

But if I lose you, what is left to hope for? What reason for continuing on the pilgrimage of life, for which I have no support but you, and none in you except the knowledge that you are alive, now that I am forbidden all other pleasures in you and denied even the joy of your presence which from time to time could restore me to myself? O God – if I dare say it -- cruel to me in everything! O merciless mercy! O Fortune who is only ill-fortune, who has already spent on me so many of the shafts she uses in her battle against mankind that she has none left with which to vent her anger on others. She has emptied a full quiver on me, so that from now on no one else need fear her onslaughts, and if she still had a single arrow she could find no place in me to take a wound. Her only dread is that through my many wounds death may end my sufferings; and though she does not cease to destroy me, she still fears the destruction which she hurries on.

Of all wretched women I am the most wretched, and amongst the unhappy I am unhappiest. The higher I was exalted when you preferred me above all other women, the greater my suffering over my own fall and yours, when I was flung down; for the higher the ascent, the heavier the fall. Has Fortune ever set any great or noble woman over me or made her my equal, only to be similarly cast down and crushed with grief? What glory she gave me in you, what ruin she brought upon me through you! Violent in either extreme, she showed no moderation in good or evil. To make me the saddest of all women she first made me blessed above all, so that when I thought how much I had lost, my consuming grief would match my crushing loss, and my sorrow for what was taken from me would be the greater for the fuller joy of possession which had gone before; and so that the happiness of supreme ecstasy would end in the supreme bitterness of sorrow.

What have you decided? What will you tell me about Switzerland? It seems to me that we could take a very good trip. On the way we could stop off at Vienna, Berlin, etc., go to the theatres. Eh? What do you think?

Savina is putting on my old skit, 'The Jubilee', at her benefit. Again they will say that this is a new play and they will gloat.

Today it's sunny, a bright day, but I sit indoors because Altschuller has forbidden me to go out. My temperature, by the way, is completely normal.

You keep writing, my own, that your conscience is tormenting you because you are living in Moscow and not with me in Yalta. Well, what can we do about it, my dear one? Judge the matter properly: if you were to stay with me in Yalta all through the winter your life would be marred and I would feel the pangs of remorse, which would hardly improve matters for us. I knew, of course, that I was marrying an actress – that is, when I married I realized clearly that you would be spending your winters in Moscow. I do not consider myself passed over or wronged one millionth of a degree – on the contrary, it seems to me that everything is going well, or the way it ought to go and so, darling, don't disconcert me by your remorse. In March we shall start living happily once more and, once more, won't be feeling the loneliness we are feeling now. Calm down, my own, don't be agitated, live, and hope. Hope, and nothing more.

The supplement to *Ploughed Land* has arrived: my short stories, with a portrait and, under the portrait, a wretchedly executed facsimile of my signature.

I am working now; probably I won't be writing you every day. Do forgive me.

Let's go abroad. Let's!

Your spouse,

A

Franz Kafka to Felice Bauer   20 December 1912

My dearest, what is it that makes you so anxious? Are we not living side by side as peacefully as is possible in this misery? What comes over you? You are at once both the quiet and the confusion of my heart; imagine my heartbeat when you are in this state. I have read your letter many times with burning cheeks in the hope that some kind of peace, some kind of gaiety, would somewhere show itself. It was surely only the mood of an unfortunate evening, and my agitated scrap from the office, which I might as well enclose, is really no longer true. For I know that tomorrow will again bring a confident letter from my strong girl, who was overcome by exhaustion and terrible torment for but a single midnight hour.

I abandoned the second daily letter with the best intentions, in the belief that we would both gain more peace and more confidence. This twice-repeated connecting, and twice-repeated breaking-up each day, was terrible for me, and persecuted and worried me incessantly all through the morning and then again all through the afternoon. This futile striving for an impossibility – i.e., your presence – must surely dismay not only me, dearest, but you as well each time it happens. But you may be right after all. Once a day I have to write to you; otherwise I would rather drop everything, otherwise I wouldn't know what to do with myself – and it wouldn't bring you any nearer; but if only it would make you feel a shade calmer, I will start writing twice again. It doesn't matter whether I am in the mood for only one letter to you, that doesn't matter; what matters is whether by writing twice a day I could still manage to summon, at least to some extent, the energy for everything else that is expected of me. Because to let this feeling of oneness with you, which I have in my innermost self, rise and hit me in the face by writing twice a day – that might be too great a risk at this sad distance at which I have to live.

But now I must be off again; I have to go and help Max with a document to be notarized. Come to think of it, it was today that you had to swear in court and had more troubles. Let me kiss you, dearest, pale, tormented child! He who signs himself below belongs to you not like an object in your room, but as you would wish it, and for ever.

Yours,

Franz

Mary Elcho to Arthur Balfour
In a train between Oxford and Warwick, 19 January 1904

I was overwhelmed with depression at leaving you Sunday night and I think you looked rather sad too which – this sounds unkind – was rather a consolation. It was horrid leaving at that hour but practically it was unavoidable so 'there's nothing to regret' in *that* since (this is a Whitt phrase) except that it had to be done and I think it was quite clever of me to fit in everything so well and manage to get to you – you see, I felt it my duty to put you in *yr place* (on yr knees at my feet) and *that* I flatter myself I have thoroughly done. Sunday was a little disappointing, because altho' my conscience wanted you to go to church I *should* have liked to have had some fun with you in the morning. I was in great spirits and full of mischief when you rushed in. (By the way, how *awful* of you to leave my letter in yr room) then came the long walk and one hour in yr room seemed very little in all the day and it was wasted in talking business. 2 hrs is what I like: one for boring things and one for putting you in yr place.

King James I to George Villiers, First Duke of Buckingham [c. 1622]

My only sweet and dear child,

I am now so miserable a coward, as I do nothing but weep and mourn; for I protest to God, I rode this afternoon a great way in the park without speaking to anybody, and the tears trickling down my cheeks, as now they do, that I can scarcely see to write. But, alas! what shall I do at our parting? The only small comfort that I can have will be to pry into thy defects with the eye of an enemy, and of every mote to make a mountain; and so harden my heart against thy absence. But this little malice is like jealousy, proceeding from a sweet root; but in one point it overcometh it, for, as it proceeds from love, so it cannot but end in love.

Sweet heart! be earnest with Kate to come and meet thee at New Hall within eight or ten days after this. Cast thee to be here tomorrow, as near as about two in the afternoon as thou canst, and come galloping hither. Remember thy picture, and suffer none of the Council to come here – for God's sake! Write not a word again, and let no creature see this letter. The Lord of heaven and earth bless thee, and my sweet daughter, and my sweet little grandchild, and all thy blessed family, and send thee a happier return – both now and thou knowest when – to thy dear dad and Christian gossip.

James R.

Bernard Shaw to Stella Campbell
Hotel Croix d'Or, Valence-sur-Rhone, 17 September 1913

I pursued the critical comparison of you with other women for some time after I entered on them in my last letter. I asked myself whether to be a frightfully wonderful virtuoso in the old art of love was greater than to be a blundering beginner in new developments. I handled the subject very coolly indeed. And then, in the evening I came out of a high and windy region into evening and an Italian valley; for though the long descent from St Agreve to Lamestre is in France, there is nothing more Italian in the world than its colour. At the first glance I melted and went to pieces; and the

Virgin's hood which crowned the mountains was *your* hood. No; I am not a sprite – at least not always.

Stella: I am horribly unhappy every morning. *Now* I am not particularly so; for this afternoon I came to a splendid 4000 foot mountain and had to drive right up it for eight mortal miles, reversing at impossible hairpin corners, and crawling so slowly that a good white horse which I passed at the foot passed me at the top when we stopped to replenish our boiled-away tank. Then came buckets of rain and an interminable drive down again on a ledge along an endless valley. After that, one is satisfied with physical labour & vigilance. But in the morning I shall be horribly unhappy again. It is not wholly the lost-dog feeling of vagabondizing, nor the hideous vicissitudes of mood which make me travel such a see saw. Oh I cant put it all down on paper: I suppose I will tell you some day.

I must leave this letter unwritten after all. Send me a scrap of news: we shall be here for the rest of the week. What is happening to *The Adored One*? I send you many wireless messages: do you ever send me any? Goodnight.

G.B.S.

Laurence Sterne to Catherine de Fourmantel
London, 176[0]

My dear Kitty,

I have arrived here safe & sound, except for the Hole in my Heart, which you have made like a dear enchanting Slut as you are. I shall take Lodgings this morning in Picadilly or the Haymarket, & before I seal this letter, will let you know where to direct a Letter to me, which Letter I shall wait for by the return of the Post with great impatience; so write, my dear Love, without fail. I have the greatest honours paid me & most civilities shewn me, that were ever known from the Great; and am engaged all ready to ten Noble Men & Men of fashion to dine. Mr Garrick pays me all & more honour than I could look for. I dined with him to-day, & he has promised Numbers of great People to carry me to dine with 'em. He has given me an Order for the Liberty of his Boxes, and of every part of his House for the whole Season; & indeed leaves nothing undone that can do me either Service or Credit; he has undertaken the management of the Booksellers, & will procure me a great price – but more of this in my next.

And now my dear, dear Girl! let me assure you of the truest friendship for you, that ever man bore towards a woman. Where ever I am, my heart is warm towards you, & ever shall be till it is cold for ever. I thank you for the kind proof you gave me of your Love, and of yr desire to make my heart easy, in ordering yr self to be denied to you know who; – whilst I am so miserable to be separated from my dear, dear Kitty, it would have stabb'd my soul to have thought such a fellow could have the Liberty of comeing near you. I therefore take this proof of your Love & good principles most kindly, & have as much faith & dependence upon you in it, as if I was at yr Elbow; – would to God I was at it this moment! but I am sitting solitary & alone in my bed Chamber (ten o'clock at night, after the Play), & would give a Guinea for a squeeze of yr hand. I send my Soul perpetually out to see what you are adoing; – wish I could send my Body with it. Adieu, dear & kind Girl! and believe me ever yr kind friend & most affte Admirer. I go to the Oratorio this night.

Adieu! Adieu!

P.S. My service to yr Mama.

Richard Steele to his wife   *30 September 1710*

Dear Prue,

I am very sleepy and tired, but could not think of closing my eyes till I had told you I am, dearest creature, your most affectionate and faithful husband,

Richard Steele

INSTRUCTION

Lucrezia Borgia to Pietro Bembo   [1517]

My dearest Misser Pietro,

I know that the very expectation of something awaited is the greater part of satisfaction because the hope of possessing it inflames desire. The rarer it is, the more beautiful it seems, the commoner, the less so. I decided to put off writing to you until this moment, so for that, by awaiting some exquisite reward to your most exquisite letters, you have become the source of your own satisfaction; you are both creditor and payer.

Nevertheless I have in two of my letter, confessed to Monsignor Thesauriero of my debt to you and this may have constituted no small part of what I can pay. As far as the rest is concerned, I do not believe that I can be held bound. In your letters you express with such ease all that you feel for me, but, I, just because I feel so well disposed towards you, am unable to do so. It is this feeling of powerlessness which absolves me from the debt. However as it would be wrong for me to be both prosecutor and judge of my own cause, I submit to the weighty judgement of the aforesaid Monsignor Thesauriero, commending myself to his Lordship and you. Ferrara the seventh day of August.

Your own Duchess of Ferrara

Ninon de l'Enclos to the Marquis de Sévigné

Shall I tell you what renders love dangerous? It is the sublime idea which one often appears to have about it. But in exact truth, Love, taken as a passion, is only a blind instinct which one must know how to value correctly; an *appetite* which determines you for one object rather than for another, without being able to give any reason for one's preference; considered as a link of friendship, when reason presides over it, it is not a passion, it is no longer love, it is an affectionate esteem, in truth, but peaceful, incapable of leading you out of bounds; when, however, you walk in the traces of our ancient heroes of romance, you go in for the grand sentiments, you will see that this pretended heroism only makes of love a deplorable and often disastrous folly. It is a true fanaticism; but if you strip it of all those virtues of hearsay, it will soon minister to your happiness and to your pleasures. Believe me, that if it were reason or enthusiasm which governed affairs of the heart, love would become either insipid or a delirium. The only way to avoid these two extremes is to follow the path I indicate to you. You have need of being amused and you will only find what you require for that amongst the women I speak of. Your heart needs occupation; they are made to captivate it...

Honesty in love, marquis! How can you think of that!

Ah, you are a good man gone wrong. I shall take great care not to show your letter; you would be dishonoured. You could not, you say, take on yourself to employ the manoeuvre which I have counselled you. Your frankness, your grandiose sentiments would have made your fortune in the old days. Then one used to treat love as a matter of honour; but today, when the corruption of the century has changed everything, Love is no more than a play of whim and vanity ... How many occasions do you not find where a lover gains as much by dissimulating the excess of his passion, as he would in others, by displaying greater passion than he feels?

John Keats to Fanny Brawne   8 July [1819]

My sweet Girl,

Your Letter gave me more delight, than any thing in the world but yourself could do; indeed I am almost astonished that any absent one should have that luxurious power over my senses which I feel. Even when I am not thinking of you I receive your influence and a tenderer nature steeling upon me. All my thoughts, my unhappiest days and nights have I find not at all cured me of my love of Beauty, but made it so intense that I am miserable that you are not with me: or rather breathe in that dull sort of patience that cannot be called Life. I never knew before, what such a love as you have made me feel, was; I did not believe in it; my Fancy was affraid of it, lest it should burn me up. But if you will fully love me, though there may be some fire, 'twill not be more than we can bear when moistened and bedewed with Pleasures. You mention 'horrid people' and ask me whether it depend upon them, whether I see you again. Do understand me, my love, in this. I have so much of you in my heart that I must turn Mentor when I see a chance of harm beffaling you. I would never see any thing but Pleasure in your eyes, love on your lips, and Happiness in your steps. I would wish to see you among those amusements suitable to your inclinations and spirits; so that our loves might be a delight in the midst of Pleasures agreeable enough, rather than a resource from vexations and cares. But I doubt much, in case of the worst, whether I shall be philosopher enough to follow my own Lessons: if I saw my resolution give you a pain I could not. Why may I not speak of your Beauty, since without that I could never have lov'd you. I cannot conceive any beginning of such love as I have for you but Beauty. There may be a sort of love for which, without the least sneer at it, I have the highest respect and can admire it in others: but it has not the richness, the bloom, the full form, the enchantment of love after my own heart. So let me speak of you[r] Beauty, though to my own endangering; if you could be so cruel to me as to try elsewhere its Power. You say you are afraid I shall think you do not love me – in saying this you make me ache the more to be near you. I am at the diligent use of my faculties here, I do not pass a day without sprawling some blank verse or tagging some rhymes; and here I must confess, that, (since I am on that subject,) I love you the more in that I believe you have liked me for my own sake and for nothing else. I have met with women whom I really think would like to be married to a Poem and to be given away by a Novel. I have seen your Comet, and only wish it was a sign that poor Rice would get well whose illness makes him rather a melancholy companion: and the more so as so to conquer his feelings and hide them from me, with a forc'd Pun. I kiss'd your writing over in the hope you had indulg'd me by leaving a trace of honey – What was your dream? Tell it me and I will tell you the interpretation thereof.

Ever yours, my love!

John Keats

Do not accuse me of delay – we have not here an opportunity of sending letters every day. Write speedily.

Walter Bagehot to Elizabeth Wilson
Herd's Hill, 22 November 1857

My dearest Eliza,

I fear you will think the answer I wrote yesterday to your most kind and *delicious* letter, was very superficial, but I wrote it at once while people were talking and bothering me. I have now read yours over and over more times than I should like to admit. I awoke in the middle of the night and immediately lit a candle to read it a few times again. It has given me more pleasure than I ever received from a letter, and infinitely more than I thought it possible I could receive from one. I fancy that it is not now an effort to you to write to me – at least it reads as if it was written without effort. Yet it tells me things which with your deep and reserved nature it must have cost you much to put on paper. I wish indeed I could feel worthy of your affection – my reason, if not my imagination, is getting to believe you when you whisper to me that I have it, but as somebody says in Miss Austen, 'I do not at all mind having what is too good for me'; my delight is at times intense. You must not suppose because I tell you of the wild, burning pain which I have felt, and at times, though I am and *ought* to be much soothed, still feel, that my love for you has ever been mere suffering. Even at the worst there was a wild, delicious excitement which I would not have lost for the world. At first, and before the feeling was very great it was simple pleasure to me to come to Claverton, and the charm of our early intellectual talks was very great, although of late, and particularly since the day in the conservatory, the feeling has been too eager not to have a good deal of pain in it, and the tension of mind has really been very great at times, still the time that I have known and loved you is immensely the happiest I have ever known. My spirits always make me cheerful in a superficial way, but they do not *satisfy*, and somehow life even before I was engaged to you was sweeter and gentler, and the jars and jangles of action lost their influence, and literature had a new value since *you* liked my writing, and everything has had a gloss upon it. Though I have come to Claverton the last few times with the notion that the gloss would go – that I should burst out and you would be tranquil and kind and considerate and *refuse* and I should never see you again. I had a vision of the thing which I keep by me. As it has *not* happened I am afraid this is egotistical – indeed I know it is – but I am not sure that egotism is bad in letters, and if I write to you I *must* write about what I feel for you. It is odd how completely our feelings change. No one can tell the effort it was to me to tell you I loved you – why I do not know, but it made me gasp for breath, and now it is absolutely pleasure to me to tell it to you and bore you with it in every form, and I should like to write it in big letters I LOVE YOU all across the page by way of emphasis. I know you will think me very childish and be shaken in your early notion that I am intellectual, but I cannot help it. This is my state of mind.

Dorothy Osborne to Sir William Temple

There are a great many ingredients must go to the making me happy in a husband. First, as my cousin Franklin says, our humours must agree; and to do that he must have that kind of breeding that I have had, and used that kind of company. That is, he must not be so much a country gentleman as to understand nothing but hawks and dogs, and be fonder of either than his wife; nor of the next sort of them whose aim reaches no further than to be Justice of the Peace, and once in his life High Sheriff, who reads no book but Statutes, and studies nothing but how to make a speech interlarded with Latin that may amaze his disagreeing poor neighbours, and fright them rather than persuade them into quietness. He must not be a thing that began the world in a free school, was sent from thence to the university, and is at his furthest when he reaches the Inns of Court, has no acquaintance but those of his form in these places, speaks the French he has picked out of old laws, and admires nothing but the stories he has heard of the revels that were kept there before his time. He must not be a town gallant neither, that lives in a tavern and an ordinary, that cannot imagine how an hour should be spent without company unless it be in sleeping, that makes court to all the women he sees, thinks they believe him, and laughs and is laughed at equally. Nor a travelled Monsieur whose head is all feather inside and outside, than can talk of nothing but dances and duets, and has courage enough to wear slashes when every one else dies with cold to see him. He must not be a fool of no sort, nor peevish, nor ill-natured, nor proud, nor covetous; and to all this must be added, that he must love me and I him as much as we are capable of loving. Without all this, his fortune, though never so great, would not satisfy me; and with it, a very moderate one would keep me from ever repenting my disposal.

Marcel Proust to Reynaldo Hahn
[18 or 20? August 1896]

Établissement Thermal & Casino, Mont-Dore
(Puy-de-Dôme)

My dear little Reynaldo,

If I don't wire, it's because in case you've left I wouldn't want them to open my telegram. And yet I'd terribly like you to know straight away. Forgive me if you're angry with me, but I'm not angry with you. Forgive me if I've hurt you, and in future don't tell me anything since it upsets you. You will never find a more affectionate, more understanding (alas!) and less humiliating confessor, since, if you had asked silence of him as he has asked a confession of you, your heart would have been the confessional and he the sinner, for that is how weak he is, weaker than you. Never mind, and forgive me for having added, out of egoism as you say, to the sorrows of your life. But how could it have been otherwise? It might be great, but it would not be natural, to live in our time as Tolstoy asks us to do. But of the substitution it would be necessary to make, the little detour, if one is at last to get back into life, I cannot speak to you, for I know you don't like it and that my words would be taken amiss. Don't worry about having grieved me. For one thing it would be only too natural. At every moment of our life we are the descendants of ourselves, and the atavism which weighs on us is our past, preserved by habit. And if bad seed has been mixed with the good, the harvest will not be entirely a happy one. 'The fathers have eaten sour grapes,' says the Bible, 'and the children's teeth are set on edge.' Actually, I'm not at all upset. No, that's wrong. I am rather upset over what's happening to Chicot; if he must die, I'd at least like the king to know all he has done for him. If I had sorrows, they would be relieved by the pleasure that Bussy is having at the moment. And my own joys or sorrows would not seem much more real to me than those of the book, to which I resign myself. So you see, I have no sorrows, only an enormous tenderness for my boy, whom I think of, as I said of my nurse when I was little, not only with all my heart, but with all me. The other day I had a letter from our dear Mlle Suzette, it was charming and of the utmost interest, as they say. But how she loves to be pitied. She told you that she hadn't let me notice her grief, but she writes to me that she conceals her distress from you. There's too much artifice in all that. One would like her to reread Vigny's 'Mort du loup'.

> *To pray, to scream, to sigh, one's as cowardly as the other*
> *... Suffer and die in silence*

(That's not quoted very accurately.) I realize that smacks of a Stoic wisdom which doesn't do anybody much good and certainly can't be expected of a young girl except in Corneille. But frankly, what do you think of this business of telling you how she hides her sorrow from me and vice versa. She strikes me as the kind of person who would turn her back to prevent you from seeing her tears but only after making sure that you'd seen them in the mirror. An artful way of arranging to be pitied for her sorrow and admired for her heroism.

Her soul isn't as base as all that, there's no great calculation in it, and I hope it's natural. But you have to admit that it comes naturally to her to be very affected. It's all so theatrical. 'Why, Mother, what's wrong?' 'Oh, nothing. A moment's weakness … the heat … these roses … oh, my dear boy, you can see that I've never been so well in all my life, that there's nothing nothing nothing wrong…' Whereupon she falls down dead, or if you prefer, 'that I've never been so happy, so gay' and she bursts out sobbing. Let us take care, my dearest, not to sympathize with grief only when it takes the forms that are congenial to us and disturb us the least, but let us never imitate theatrical display and the artificial demonstration of often imaginary sorrows. I didn't wire you that I was coming home tomorrow for fear of preventing you from going to Villers. Just as well, for I may stick it out in spite of Mama's discouragement and determination to take me home. We were wrong in condemning this treatment. The trouble is that they are haymaking all round here. You know Mme de Sévigné too well not to know all about haying. It's lovely but bad for me. Mme Conneau was here, we were both invited to dinner by a Dr Schlemmer, to whom Hillemacher dedicated a melody and who has studied harmony. I have no great faith in him but he's very intelligent. He is not my doctor here. I'm in the middle of the second volume of *La Dame de Monsoreau* and I'm also getting on, but more slowly, with Rousseau's *Confessions.* Today I'm all music, I'd like to hear you sing

The invisible hand of the saints

and many other things.

You must have received three copies of *Les Plaisirs et les jours,* one for you (which is not a present, I told Calmann to send it to you at his expense), one for your sister Elisa, and one for your cousin. I have been working a little in the last two days. I haven't come to any decision about my 28 days. Tell me in your next letter if, after what I've said, you consent to be released from your little oaths, and if in September you would like to go to Switzerland or somewhere else. Otherwise, even apart from the 28 days, I may spend September in Versailles, but not because of you, bad boy, it won't bind you in any way. What a lot of pages! and I haven't said anything yet about the little Baudelaire book. That will have to wait till next time. And have you received the appendix to Mme de Sévigné with the facsimiles?

I embrace you tenderly, your sisters too, except the one with the jealous husband. I, who am no longer jealous but have been, respect jealous people and have no wish to cause them the slightest unhappiness or to lead them to suspect any secret.

Marcel

Sylvia Townsend Warner to David Garnett
18 June 1973

Dearest David,

... Tiber makes love to you for the good reason that he loves you, and loves making love. Cats are passionate and voluptuous, they get satisfaction from mating but no pleasure (the females dislike it, and this is wounding to the male), no voluptuousness; *and no appreciation.* Tiber has the pleasure of being pleased and knowing he pleases in his love-making with you. I am so glad you have each other. Does he roll on his head? Does he fall asleep with an ownerly paw laid over you?

We had a dark grey cat (Norfolk bred, very Norfolk in character) called Tom. He was reserved, domineering, voluptuous – much as I imagine Tiber to be. When he was middle-aged he gave up nocturnal prowlings and slept on my bed, against my feet. One evening I was reading in bed when I became aware that Tom was staring at me. I put down my book, said nothing, watched. Slowly, with a look of intense concentration, he got up and advanced on me, like Tarquin with ravishing strides, poised himself, put out a front paw, and stroked my cheek as I used to stroke his chops. A human caress from a cat. I felt very meagre and ill-educated that I could not purr.

It had never occurred to me that their furry love

develops from what was shown them as kittens. I expect you are right. The ownerly paw is certainly a nursing cat's gesture.

You should encourage Tiber to sleep with you. He might come to prefer it to midnight battling with the Wood Cat. Come winter, he certainly will. I am afraid of the Wood Cat's claws, still more of his teeth.

Were your hailstones blue? We once had such a storm here, with lightning ripping hail from the sky; and the hailstones were hard as marbles, and blue as aquamarines. And there was another storm, after a long drought, when the lightning was green. It was strange to see the bleached fields, the rusty trees, momentarily sluiced with the look of spring.

I have been spared acquaintances who might have explained to me about blue hailstones and green lightning, so I can enjoy them with simple pleasure.

> Earth, that grew with joyful ease
> Hemlock for Socrates –

The longer I live, the more my heart assents to that couplet.

With love

Sylvia

Your favor of Aug. the 19., my very dear friend, is put into my hands this 26th. day of September 1788. and I answer it in the same instant to shew you there is nothing nearer my heart than to meet all the testimonies of your esteem. It is a strong one that you will occupy yourself for me on such a trifle as a visiting card. But sketch it only with your pencil, my friend, and do not make of it a serious business. This would render me uneasy, because I did not mean such a trespass on your time. A few strokes of your pencil on a card will be enjoiment enough for me.

I am going to America, and you to Italy. The one or the other of us goes the wrong way, for the way will ever be wrong which leads us farther apart. Mine is a journey of duty and of affection. I must deposit my daughters in the bosom of their friends and country. This done, I shall return to my station. My absence may be as short as five months, and certainly not longer than nine. How long my subsequent stay here may be I cannot tell. It would certainly be the longer had I a single friend here like yourself. – In going to Italy, be sure to cross the Alps at the Col de Tende. It is the best pass, because you need never get out of your carriage. It is practicable in seasons when all the other passes are shut up by snow. The roads leading to and from it are as fine as can possibly be, and you will see the castle of Saorgio. Take a good day for that part of your journey, and when you shall have sketched it in your portefeuille, and copied it more at leisure for yourself, tear out the leaf and send it to me. But why go to Italy? You have seen it, all the world has seen it, and ransacked it thousands of times. Rather join our good friend Mrs Church in her trip to America. There you will find original scenes, scenes worthy of your pencil, such as the Natural bridge or the Falls of Niagara. Or participate with Trumbull the historical events of that country. These will have the double merit of being new, and of coming from you. I should find excuses for being sometimes of your parties. Think of this, my dear friend, mature the project with Mrs Church, and let us all embark together at Havre. Adieu ma tres chere et excellente amie. Your's affectionately,

Th: J

Mozart to his wife   Dresden, 16 April 1789

Dear little wife, I have a number of requests to make. I beg you

(1) not to be melancholy,

(2) to take care of your health and to beware of the spring breezes,

(3) not to go out walking alone – and preferably not to go out walking at all,

(4) to feel absolutely assured of my love. Up to the present I have not written a single letter to you without placing your dear portrait before me.

(6) and lastly I beg you to send me more details in your letters. I should very much like to know whether our brother-in-law Hofer came to see us the day after my departure? Whether he comes very often, as he promised me he would? Whether the Langes come sometimes? Whether progress is being made with the portrait? What sort of life you are leading? All these things are naturally of great interest to me.

(5) I beg in your conduct not only to be careful of your honour and mine, but also to consider appearances. Do not be angry with me for asking this. You ought to love me even more for thus valuing our honour [last two paragraphs thus reversed in copy of letter in Berlin Library].

W. A. Mozart

Mozart to his wife   Vienna, 11 June 1791

... I must hurry, as it is already a quarter to seven – and the coach leaves at seven. When you are bathing, do take care not to slip and never stay in alone. If I were you I should occasionally omit a day in order not to do the cure too violently. I trust that someone slept with you last night. I cannot tell you what I would not give to be with you at Baden instead of being stuck here. From sheer boredom I composed to-day an aria for my opera. I got up as early as half-past four. Wonderful to relate, I have got back my watch – but – as I have no key, I have unfortunately not been able to wind it. What a nuisance! Schlumbla! That is a word to ponder on. Well, I wound our big clock instead. *Adieu* – my love! I am lunching to-day with Puchberg. I kiss you a thousand times and say with you in thought: 'Death and despair were his reward!'

Ever your loving husband

W. A. Mozart

See that Karl behaves himself. Give him kisses from me.

Take an electuary if you are constipated – not otherwise.

REFLECTION

John Keats to Fanny Brawne
Thursday 1 July 1819, Shanklin, Isle of Wight

My dearest Lady,

... Ask yourself my love whether you are not very cruel to have so entrammelled me, so destroyed my freedom. Will you confess this in the Letter you must write immediately and do all you can to console me in it – make it rich as a draught of poppies to intoxicate me – write the softest words and kiss them that I may at least touch my lips where yours have been. For myself I know not how to express my devotion to so fair a form: I want a brighter word than bright, a fairer word than fair. I almost wish we were butterflies and liv'd but three summer days – three such days with you I could fill with more delight than fifty common years could ever contain. But however selfish I may feel, I am sure I could never act selfishly: as I told you a day or two before I left Hampstead, I will never return to London if my Fate does not turn up Pam [the knave of clubs] or at least a Court-card. Though I could centre my Happiness in you, I cannot expect to engross your heart so entirely – indeed if I thought you felt as much for me as I do for you at this moment I do not think I could restrain myself from seeing you again tomorrow for the delight of one embrace. But no – I must live upon hope and Chance. In case of the worst that can happen, I shall still love you – but what hatred I shall have for another!

Gustave Flaubert to Louise Colet
Croisset, Friday 10 p.m., 18 September 1846

You tell me, my angel, that I have not initiated you into my inner life, into my most secret thoughts. Do you know what is most intimate, most hidden, in my heart, and what is most authentically myself? Two or three modest ideas about art, lovingly brooded over; that is all. The greatest events of my life have been a few thoughts, a few books, certain sunsets on the beach at Trouville, and talks five or six hours long with a friend now married and lost to me. I have always seen life differently from others, and the result has been that I've always isolated myself (but not sufficiently, alas!) in a state of harsh unsociability, with no exit. I suffered so many humiliations, I so shocked people and made them indignant, that I long ago came to realize that in order to live in peace one must live alone and seal one's windows lest the air of the world seep in. In spite of myself I still retain something of this habit. That is why I deliberately avoided the company of women for several years. I wanted no hindrance to my innate moral precept. I wanted no yoke, no influence. In the end I no longer desired women's company at all. Stirrings of the flesh, throbbings of the heart, were absent from my life, and I was not even conscious of my sex. As I told you, I had an overwhelming passion when I was little more than a child. When it ended I decided to divide my life in two parts: to put on one side my soul, which I reserved for Art, and on the other my body, which was to live as best it could. Then you came along and upset all that. So here I am, returning to a human existence!

You have awakened all that was slumbering, or perhaps decaying, within me! I have been loved before, and intensely, though I'm one of those who are quickly forgotten and more apt to kindle emotion than to keep it alive. The love I arouse is always that felt for something a little strange. Love, after all, is only a superior kind of curiosity, an appetite for the unknown that makes you bare your breast and plunge headlong into the storm.

As I said, I have been loved before, but *never the way you love me*; nor has there ever been between a woman and myself the bond that exists between us two. I have never felt for any woman so deep a devotion, so irresistible an attraction; never has there been such complete communion. Why do you keep saying that I love the tinselly, the showy, the flashy? 'Poet of form!' That is the favourite term of abuse hurled by utilitarians at true artists. For my part, until someone comes along and separates for me the form and the substance of a given sentence, I shall continue to maintain that that distinction is meaningless. Every beautiful thought has a beautiful form, and vice versa. In the world of Art, beauty is a by-product of form, just as in our world temptation is a by-product of love. Just as you cannot remove from a physical body the qualities that constitute it – colour, extension, solidity – without reducing it to a hollow abstraction, without destroying it, so you cannot remove the form from the Idea, because the Idea exists only by virtue of its form. Imagine an idea that has no form – such a thing is as impossible as a form that expresses no idea. Such are the stupidities on which criticism feeds. Good stylists are reproached for neglecting the Idea, the moral goal; as though the goal of the doctor were not to heal, the goal of the painter to paint, the goal of the nightingale to sing, as though the goal of Art were not, first and foremost, Beauty!

Vita Sackville-West to Violet Trefusis   3 September 1950

My darling,

It was a real event in my life and my heart to be with you the other day. We do matter to each other, don't we? however much our ways may have diverged. I think we have got something indestructible between us, haven't we? Even right back to the library seat in your papa's room at Grosvenor Street – and then at Duntreath – and then to everything that came afterwards. *Glissons, mortels* ... but what a bond, Lushka darling; a bond of childhood and subsequent passion, such as neither of us will ever share with anyone else.

It has been a very strange relationship, ours; unhappy at times, happy at others; but unique in its way, and infinitely precious to me and (may I say?) to you.

What I like about it is that we always come together again however long the gaps in our meetings may have been. Time seems to make no difference. This is a sort of love letter I suppose. Odd that I should be writing you a love letter after all these years – when we have written so many to each other. *Parceque c'était lui, parceque c'était moi.*

Oh, you sent me a book about Elizabeth Barrett Browning. Thank you, darling generous Lushka and you gave me a coal-black briquet. It lights up into the flame of love which always burns in my heart whenever I think of you. You said it would last for three months, but our love has lasted for forty years and more.

Your Mitya

Oscar Wilde to Lord Alfred Douglas
Courtfield Gardens, 20 May 1895

My child,

Today it was asked to have the verdicts rendered separately. Taylor is probably being judged at this moment, so that I have been able to come back here. My sweet rose, my delicate flower, my lily of lilies, it is perhaps in prison that I am going to test the power of love. I am going to see if I cannot make the bitter warders sweet by the intensity of the love I bear you. I have had moments when I thought it would be wiser to separate. Ah! moments of weakness and madness! Now I see that that would have mutilated my life, ruined my art, broken the musical chords which make a perfect soul. Even covered with mud I shall praise you, from the deepest abysses I shall cry to you. In my solitude you will be with me. I am determined not to revolt but to accept every outrage through devotion to love, to let my body be dishonoured so long as my soul may always keep the image of you. From your silken hair to your delicate feet you are perfection to me. Pleasure hides love from us, but pain reveals it in its essence. O dearest of created things, if someone wounded by silence and solitude comes to you, dishonoured, a laughing-stock, Oh! you can close his wounds by touching them and restore his soul which unhappiness had for a moment smothered. Nothing will be difficult for you then, and remember, it is that hope which makes me live, and that hope alone. What wisdom is to the philosopher, what God is to his saint, you are to me. To keep you in my soul, such is the goal of this pain which men call life. O my love, you whom I cherish above all things, white narcissus in an unmown field, think of the burden which falls to you, a burden which love alone can make light. But be not saddened by that, rather be happy to have filled with an immortal love the soul of a man who now weeps in hell, and yet carries heaven in his heart. I love you, I love you, my heart is a rose which your love has brought to bloom, my life is a desert fanned by the delicious breeze of your breath, and whose cool spring are your eyes; the imprint of your little feet makes valleys of shade for me, the odour of your hair is like myrrh, and wherever you go you exhale the perfumes of the cassia tree.

Love me always, love me always. You have been the supreme, the perfect love of my life; there can be no other.

I decided that it was nobler and more beautiful to stay. We could not have been together. I did not want to be called a coward or a deserter. A false name, a disguise, a hunted life, all that is not for me, to whom you have been revealed on that high hill where beautiful things are transfigured.

O sweetest of all boys, most loved of all loves, my soul clings to your soul, my life is your life, and in all the world of pain and pleasure you are my ideal of admiration and joy.

Oscar

Dorothy Osborne to Sir William Temple   [*c. 1652–4*]

Sir,

Having tired myself with thinking, I mean to weary you with reading, and revenge myself that way for all the unquiet thoughts you have given me. But I intended this a sober letter, and therefore, *sans raillerie*, let me tell you, I have seriously considered all our misfortunes, and can see no end of them but by submitting to that which we cannot avoid, and by yielding to it break the force of a blow which if resisted brings a certain ruin. I think I need not tell you how dear you have been to me, nor that in your kindness I placed all the satisfaction of my life; 'twas the only happiness I proposed to myself, and had set my heart so much upon it that it was therefore made my punishment, to let me see that, how innocent soever I thought my affection, it was guilty in being greater than is allowable for things of this world. 'Tis not a melancholy humour gives me these apprehensions and inclinations, nor the persuasions of others; 'tis the result of a long strife with myself, before my reason could overcome my passion, or bring me to a perfect resignation to whatsoever is allotted for me. 'Tis now done, I hope, and I have nothing left but to persuade you to that, which I assure myself your own judgment will approve in the end, and your reason has often prevailed with you to offer; that which you would have done then out of kindness to me and point of honour, I would have you do now out of wisdom and kindness to yourself. Not that I would disclaim my part in it or lessen my obligation to you, no, I am your friend as much as ever I was in my life, I think more, and am sure I shall never be less. I have known you long enough to discern that you have all the qualities that make an excellent friend, and I shall endeavour to deserve that you may be so to me; but I would have you do this upon the justest grounds, and such as may conduce most to your quiet and future satisfaction. When we have tried all ways to happiness, there is no such thing to be found but in a mind conformed to one's condition, whatsoever it be, and in not aiming at anything that is either impossible or improbable; all the rest is but vanity and vexation of spirit, and I durst pronounce it so from that little knowledge I have had of the world, though I had not Scripture for my warrant. The shepherd that bragged to the traveller, who asked him. 'What weather it was like to be?' that it should be what weather pleased God, and what pleased God should please him, said an excellent thing in rude language, and knew enough to make him the happiest person in the world if he made a right use on't. There can be no pleasure in a struggling life, and that folly which we condemn in an ambitious man, that's ever labouring for that which is hardly got and more uncertainly kept, is seen in all according to their several humours; in some 'tis covetousness, in others pride, in some a stubbornness of nature that chooses to go always against the tide, and in others an unfortunate fancy to things that are in themselves innocent till we make them otherwise by desiring them too much. Of this sort I think you, and I, are; we have lived hitherto upon hopes so airy that I have often wondered how they could support the weight of our misfortunes; but passion gives a strength above nature, we see it in mad people; and, not to flatter ourselves, ours is but a refined degree of madness. What can it be else to be lost to all things in the world but that single object that takes up one's fancy, to lose all the quiet and repose of one's life in hunting after it, when there is so little likelihood of ever gaining it, and so many more probable accidents that will infallibly make us miss of it? And, which is more than all, 'tis being mastered by that which reason and religion teaches us to govern, and in that only gives us a pre-eminence above beasts. This, soberly consider'd, is enough to let us see our error, and consequently to persuade us to redeem it. To another person, I should justify myself that 'tis not a lightness in my nature, nor any interest that is not common to us both, that has wrought this change in me. To you that know my heart, and from whom I shall never hide it, to whom a thousand testimonies of my kindness can witness the reality of it, and whose friendship is not built upon common grounds, I have no more to say but that I impose not my opinions upon you, and that I had rather you took them up as your own choice than upon my entreaty. But if, as we have not differed in anything else, we could agree in this too, and resolve upon a friendship that will be much the perfecter for having nothing of passion in it, how happy might we be without so much as a fear of the change that any accident could bring. We might defy all that fortune could do, and putting off all disguise and constraint, with that which only made it necessary, make our lives as easy to us as the condition of this world will permit. I may own you as a person that I extremely value and esteem, and for whom I have a particular friendship, and you may consider me as one that will always be

Your faithful

You say you want to talk to me about death: my views about death are bright, brisk and entertaining. When Azrael takes a soul it may be to other and brighter worlds: like those whither you and I go together. The transformation called Death may be something as beautiful and dazzling as the transformation called Love. It may make the dead man 'happy', just as your mother knows that you are happy. But none the less it is a transformation, and sad sometimes for those left behind. A mother whose child is dying can hardly believe that in the inscrutable Unknown there is anyone who can look to it as well as she. And if a mother cannot trust her child easily to God Almighty, shall I be so mean as to be angry because she cannot trust it easily to me? I tell you I have stood before your mother and felt like a thief. I know you are not going to part: neither physically, mentally, morally nor spiritually. But she sees a new element in your life, wholly from outside – is it not natural, given her temperament, that you should find her perturbed? Oh, dearest, dearest Frances, let us always be very gentle to older people. Indeed, darling, it is not they who are the tyrants, but we. They may interrupt our building in the scaffolding stages: we turn their house upside down when it is their final home and rest. Your mother would certainly have worried if you had been engaged to the Archangel Michael (who, indeed, is bearing his disappointment very well): how much more when you are engaged to an aimless, tactless, reckless, unbrushed, strange-hatted, opinionated scarecrow who has suddenly walked into the vacant place. I could have prophesied her unrest: wait and she will calm down all right, dear. God comfort her: I dare not...

CONFESSION

Edith Wharton to W. Morton Fullerton
early March 1908

58 Rue de Varenne

Dear, Remember, please, how impatient & anxious I shall be to know the sequel of the Bell letter . . .

— Do you know what I was thinking last night, when you asked me, & I couldn't tell you? — Only that the way you've spent your emotional life, while I've — bien malgré moi — hoarded mine, is what puts the great gulf between us, & sets us not only on opposite shores, but at hopelessly distant points of our respective shores . . . Do you see what I mean?

And I'm so afraid that the treasures I long to unpack for you, that have come to me in magic ships from enchanted islands, are only, to you, the old familiar red calico & beads of the clever trader, who has had dealings in every latitude, & knows just what to carry in the hold to please the simple native — I'm so afraid of this, that often & often I stuff my shining treasures back into their box, lest I should see you smiling at them!

Well! And if you do? It's *your* loss, after all! and if you can't come into the room without my feeling all over me a ripple of flame, & if, wherever you touch me, a heart beats under your touch, & if, when you hold me, & I don't speak, it's because all the words in me seem to have become throbbing pulses, & all my thoughts are a great golden blur – why should I be afraid of your smiling at me, when I can turn the beads & calico back into such beauty –?

Marcel Proust to Antoine Bibesco [1904]

My dear Antoine,

I am writing to you out of an exaggerated sense of conscience – and the fear of continuing to be dishonest in simply replacing with a different feeling one whose expression can persist in the other person's mind as the statement of a constant truth – (what style). It is unpleasant for me to write this to you, and moreover it is perhaps not even true, if you are to understand by 'true' something definitive, whereas what we have here is in the process of becoming truth etc. I wanted to tell you that your new attitude towards me (which is, by the way, quite understandable) – a lack of frankness, or rather an unwillingness to share confidences or ask questions, in a word, an avoidance of intimacy – has touched on something within me which did not exist before I knew you, which you have moulded, and which had grown into the habit of no longer living autonomously, stretching the horizons of its existence until they reached the boundaries of another being and so continuously dissipating in this imperceptible extension of itself the potential of its life for unfolding admirable or unworthy acts as they happened, along with the reflection of the dramas which it had chanced upon, and the secrets which had been entrusted to it. Now, having lost my second ego (that is, you) as a result of this new attitude of yours, I have been unable to alter the shape which you have given the first (my own). And just as a river whose natural progress is dammed up with a high and impenetrable barrier will run in another direction in obedience to the physical law of its flow, thereby to run to waste or to make fertile new ground, so I have had to pour out to another those confidences which you no longer wished to receive, and have had to receive from this confidant the secrets which have become essential to me since you have accustomed me to them. Enough: it makes me blush with shame that I have allowed these confessions to slip out.

Yours,

Marcel

Gustave Flaubert to Louise Colet
Croisset, 6–7 August 1846

I owe you a frank explanation of myself, in response to a page of your letter which makes me see that you harbour illusions about me. It would be cowardly of me (and cowardice is a vice that disgusts me, in whatever aspect it shows itself) to allow these to persist.

My basic character, whatever anyone may say, is that of the mountebank. In my childhood and my youth I was wildly in love with the stage. I should perhaps have been a great actor if I had happened to be born poorer. Even now, what I love above all else, is *form*, provided it be beautiful, and nothing beyond it. Women whose hearts are too ardent and whose minds too exclusive do not understand this religion of beauty, beauty considered apart from emotion. They always demand a cause, an end. I admire tinsel as much as gold: indeed, the poetry of tinsel is even greater, because it is sadder. The only things that exist for me in the world are splendid poetry, harmonious, well-turned, singing sentences, beautiful sunsets, moonlight, pictures, ancient sculpture, and strongly marked faces. Beyond that, nothing. I would rather have been Talma than Mirabeau, because he lived in a sphere of purer beauty. I am as sorry for caged birds as for enslaved human beings. In all of politics, there is only one thing that I understand: the riot. I am as fatalistic as a Turk, and believe that whether we do everything we can for the progress of humanity, or nothing at all, makes no whit of difference. As for that 'progress', I have but an obtuse comprehension of muddy ideas. I am completely out of patience with everything pertaining to that kind of language.

170

I despise modern tyranny because it seems to me stupid, weak, and without the courage of its convictions. But I have a deep cult of ancient tyranny, which I regard as mankind's finest manifestation. I am above all a man of fantasy, caprice, lack of method. I thought long and *very seriously* (don't laugh, it is a memory of my best hours) of becoming a Mohammedan in Smyrna. The day will come when I will go and settle somewhere far from here, and nothing more will be heard of me. As for what ordinarily touches men most closely, and for me is secondary – I mean physical love – I have always kept it separate from this other. I heard you jeer at J.J. on this account the other day: his case is mine exactly. You are the only woman whom I have both loved and possessed. Until now I used women to satisfy desires aroused in me by other women. You made me untrue to my system, to my heart, perhaps to my nature, which, incomplete in itself, always seeks the incomplete.

Franz Kafka to Felice Bauer   1 November 1912

Dear Fräulein Felice,

You must not take offence at this form of address, at least not this time, for if I am to write about my mode of life, as you have asked me to do several times, I shall probably have some delicate things to say which I could hardly utter to a 'Fräulein Bauer'. Moreover this new form of address cannot be so very bad, or I should not have thought it out with so much and such lasting satisfaction.

My life consists, and basically always has consisted, of attempts at writing, mostly unsuccessful. But when I didn't write, I was at once flat on the floor, fit for the dustbin. My energies have always been pitifully weak; even though I didn't quite realize it, it soon became evident that I had to spare myself on all sides, renounce a little everywhere, in order to retain just enough strength for what seemed to be my main purpose. When I didn't do so (oh God, even on a holiday such as this, when I am acting as duty officer, there is no peace, just visitor after visitor, like a little hell let loose) but tried to reach beyond my strength, I was automatically forced back, wounded, humbled, forever weakened; yet this very fact which made me temporarily unhappy is precisely what gave me confidence in the long run, and I began to think that somewhere, however difficult to find, there must be a lucky star under which it would be possible to go on living. I once drew up a detailed list of the things I have sacrificed to writing, as well as the things that were taken from me for the sake of writing, or rather whose loss was only made bearable by this explanation.

Just as I am thin, and I am the thinnest person I know

(and that's saying something, for I am no stranger to sanatoria), there is also nothing to me which, in relation to writing, one could call superfluous, superfluous in the sense of overflowing. If there is a higher power that wishes to use me, or does use me, then I am at its mercy, if no more than as a well-prepared instrument. If not, I am nothing, and will suddenly be abandoned in a dreadful void.

Now I have expanded my life to accommodate my thoughts about you, and there is hardly a quarter of an hour of my waking time when I haven't thought about you, and many quarter-hours when I do nothing else. But even this is related to my writing, my life is determined by nothing but the ups and downs of writing, and certainly during a barren period I should never have had the courage to turn to you. This is just as true as it is true that since that evening I have felt as though I had an opening in my chest through which there was an unrestrained drawing-in and drawing-out until one evening in bed, when, by calling to mind a story from the Bible, the necessity of this sensation, as well as the truth of the Bible story, were simultaneously confirmed.

Lately I have found to my amazement how intimately you have now become associated with my writing, although until recently I believed that the only time I did not think about you at all was while I was writing.

In one short paragraph I had written, there were, among others, the following references to you and your letters: someone was given a bar of chocolate. There was talk of small diversions someone had during working hours. Then there was a telephone call. And finally somebody urged someone to go to bed, and threatened to take him straight to his room if he did not obey, which was certainly prompted by the recollection of your mother's annoyance when you stayed so late at the office. – Such passages are especially dear to me; in them I take hold of you, without your feeling it, and therefore without your having to resist. And even if you were to read some of my writings, these little details would surely escape you. But believe me, probably nowhere in the world could you let yourself be caught with greater unconcern than here.

My mode of life is devised solely for writing, and if there are any changes, then only for the sake of perhaps fitting in better with my writing; for time is short, my strength is limited, the office is a horror, the apartment is noisy, and if a pleasant, straightforward life is not possible then one must try to wriggle through by subtle manoeuvres. The satisfaction gained by manoeuvring one's timetable successfully cannot be compared to the permanent misery of knowing that fatigue of any kind shows itself better and more clearly in writing than anything one is really trying to say. For the past six weeks, with some interruptions in the last few days, due to unbearable weakness, my timetable has been as follows: from 8 to 2 or 2.30 in the office, then lunch till 3 or 3.30, after that sleep in bed (usually only attempts: for a whole week I saw nothing but Montenegrins in my sleep, in extremely disagreeable clarity, which gave me headaches, I saw every detail of their complicated dress) till 7.30, then ten minutes of exercises, naked at the open window, then an hour's walk – alone, with Max, or with another friend, then dinner with my family (I have three sisters, one married, one engaged; the single one, without prejudicing my affection for the others, is easily my favourite); then at 10.30 (but often not till 11.30) I sit down to write, and I go on, depending on my strength, inclination, and luck, until 1, 2, or 3 o'clock, once even till 6 in the morning. Then again exercises, as above, but of course avoiding all exertions, a wash, and then, usually with a slight pain in my heart and twitching stomach muscles, to bed. Then every imaginable effort to get to sleep – i.e., to achieve the impossible, for one cannot sleep (Herr K. even demands dreamless sleep) and at the same time be thinking about one's work and trying to solve with certainty the one question that certainly is insoluble, namely, whether there will be a letter from you the next day, and at what time. Thus the night consists of two parts: one wakeful, the other sleepless, and if I were to tell you about it at length and you were prepared to listen, I should never finish. So it is hardly surprising if, at the office the next morning, I only just manage to start work with what little strength is left. In one of the corridors along which I always walk to reach my typist, there used to be a coffin-like trolley for the moving of files and documents, and each time I passed it I felt as though it had been made for me, and was waiting for me.

To be precise, I must not forget that I am not only a clerk, but also a manufacturer. For my brother-in-law owns an asbestos factory, and I (although only through money my father put into it) am a partner, and as such am on the board. This factory has already caused me enough pain and worry, but I don't want to talk about that now; in any case, I have neglected it for some time (i.e., I withhold my anyway useless collaboration) as much as I can, and more or less get by with it.

Once again I have told you so little, and have asked no questions, and once again I must close. But not a single answer and, even more certainly, not a single question shall be lost. There exists some kind of sorcery by which two people, without seeing each other, without talking to each other, can at least discover the greater part about each other's past, literally in a flash, without having to tell each other all and everything; but this, after all, is almost an instrument of black magic (without seeming to be) which, although never without reward, one would certainly never resort to with impunity. Therefore I won't say it, unless you guess it first. It is terribly short, like all magic formulas. Farewell, and let me reinforce this greeting by lingering over your hand.

Yours,

Franz K.

Dora Carrington to Lytton Strachey
Saturday morning, 12 o'ck [14 May 1921]

The Mill House, Tidmarsh

My dearest Lytton,

There is a great deal to say and I feel very incompetent to write it today. Last night I composed a great many letters to you, almost till three in the morning. I then wrote an imaginary letter and bared my very soul to you. This morning I don't feel so intimate. *You* mayn't value my pent up feelings and a tearful letter. *I* rather object to them not being properly received and left about. Well there was more of a crisis than I thought when I wrote to you on Thursday. Ralph had one of his break downs and completely collapsed. He threw himself in the Woolves' arms and asked their sympathy and advice. Leonard and Virginia both said it was hopeless for him to go on as he was, that he must either marry me, or leave me completely. He came down to Reading yesterday and met me at the Coffee tea shop. He looked dreadfully ill and his mouth twitched. I'd really made my mind up some time ago that if it came to the ultimate point, I would give in. Only typically I preferred to defer it indefinitely and avoid it if possible. You see I knew there was nothing really to hope for from you – Well ever since the beginning. Then Alix told me last spring what you told James. That you were slightly terrified of my becoming dependent on you, and a permanent limpet and other things. I didn't tell you, because after all, it is no use having scenes. But you must know Ralph repeated every word you once told him in bed; that night when we were all three together. The next day we went for a walk on the Swindon downs. Perhaps you remember. I shall never forget that spot of ground, just outside Chisledon, at the foot of the downs, when he repeated every word you had said. He told me of course because he was jealous and wanted to hurt me. But it altered things, because ever after that I had a terror of being physically on your nerves and revolting you. I never came again to your bedroom. Why am I raking all this up now? Only to tell you that all these years I have known all along that my life with you was limited. I could never hope for it to become permanent. After all Lytton, you are the only person who I have ever had an all absorbing passion for. I shall never have another. I couldn't now. I had one of the most self abasing loves that a person can have. You could throw me into transports of happiness and dash me into deluges of tears and despair, all by a few words. But these aren't reproaches. For after all it's getting on for 6 years since I first met you at Asheham; and that's a long time to be happy. And I know we shall always be friends now until I die. Of course these years of Tidmarsh when we were quite alone will always be the happiest I ever spent. And I've such a store of good things which I've saved up, that I feel I could never be lonely again now. Still it's too much of a strain to be quite alone here waiting to see you or craning my nose and eyes out of the top window at 41 Gordon Square to see if you are coming down the street, when I know we'll be better friends, if you aren't haunted by the idea that I am sitting depressed in some corner of the world waiting for your footstep. It's slightly mythical of course. I can pull myself together if I want to and I am more aware than you think, the moment I am getting on your nerves and when I am not wanted. I saw the relief you felt at Ralph taking me away, so to speak, off your hands. I think he'll make me happier, than I should be entirely by myself and it certainly prevents me becoming morbid about you. And as Ralph said last night you'll never leave us. Because in spite of our dullnesses, nobody loves you nearly as much as we do. So in the café

179

in that vile city of Reading, I said I'd marry him. And now he's written to his father and told him. After all I don't believe it will make much difference and to see him so happy is a rather definite thing. I'd probably never marry anyone else and I doubt if a kinder creature exists on this earth. Last night in bed he told me everything Virginia and Leonard had told him. Again a conversation you had with them was repeated to me. Ralph was so happy he didn't hear me gasp and as it was dark he didn't see the tears run down my cheeks. Virginia told him that you had told them you didn't intend to come to Tidmarsh much after Italy and you were nervous lest I'd feel I had a sort of claim on you if I lived with [you] for a long time, ten years and that they all wondered how you could have stood me so long and how on earth we lived together alone here, as I didn't understand a word of literature and we had nothing in common intellectually or physically. That was wrong. For nobody I think could have loved the Ballades, Donne, and Macaulay's Essays and best of all, Lytton's Essays, as much as I. Virginia then told him that she thought I was still in love with you. Ralph asked me if I was. I said I didn't think perhaps I was as much as I used to be. So now I shall never tell *you* I do care again. It goes after today somewhere deep down inside me and I'll not resurrect it to hurt either you, or Ralph. Never again. He knows I am not in love with him. But he feels my affections are great enough to make him happy if I live with him. I cried last night Lytton, whilst he slept by my side sleeping happily. I cried to think of a savage cynical fate which had made it impossible for my love ever to be used by you. You never knew, or never will know the very big and devastating love I had for you. How I adored every hair, every curl on your beard. How I devoured you whilst you read to me at night. How I loved the smell of your face in your sponge. Then the ivory skin on your hands, your voice, and your hat when I saw it coming along the top of the garden wall from my window. Say you will remember it, that it wasn't all lost and that you'll forgive me for this out burst, and always be my friend. Just thinking of you now makes me cry so I can't see this paper, and yet so happy that the next moment I am calm. I shall be with you in Italy in two weeks, how lovely that will be. And this summer we shall all be very happy together. Please never show this letter to anyone. Ralph is such a dear, I don't feel I'll ever regret marrying him. Though I never will change my maiden name that I have kept for so long – so you mayn't ever call me anything but Carrington. . .

Lord Byron to Augusta Leigh   Venice, 17 May 1819

My dearest Love,

I have been negligent in not writing, but what can I say. Three years absence – & the total change of scene and habit make such a difference – that we have now nothing in common but our affections and our relationship.

But I have never ceased nor can cease to feel for a moment that perfect and boundless attachment which bound & binds me to you – which renders me utterly incapable of *real* love for any other human being – what could they be to me after *you*? My own xxx [short word crossed out] we may have been very wrong – but I repent of nothing except that cursed marriage – & your refusing to continue to love me as you had loved me – I can neither forget nor quite *forgive you* for that precious piece of reformation – but I can never be other than I have been – and whenever I love anything it is because it reminds me in some way or other of yourself – for instance I not long ago attached myself to a Venetian for no earthly reason (although a pretty woman) but because she was called xxxx [short word crossed out] and she often remarked (without knowing the reason) how fond I was of the name. – It is heart-breaking to think of our long Separation – and I am sure more than punishment enough for all our sins – Dante is more humane in his 'Hell' for he places his unfortunate lovers (Francesca of Rimini & Paolo whose case fell a good deal short of *ours* – though sufficiently naughty) in company – and though they suffer – it is at least together. – If ever I return to England – it will be to see you – and recollect that in all time – & place – and feelings – I have never ceased to be the same to you in heart – Circumstances may have ruffled my manner – & hardened my spirit – you may have seen me harsh & exasperated with all things around me; grieved & tortured with *your new resolution,* – & the soon after persecution of that infamous fiend who drove me from my Country & conspired against my life – by endeavouring to deprive me of all that could render it precious – but remember that even then *you* were the sole object that cost me a tear? and *what tears*! do you remember *our* parting? I have not spirits now to write to you upon other subjects – I am well in health – and have no cause of grief but the reflection that we are not together – When you write to me speak to me of yourself – & say that you love me – never mind common-place people & topics – which can be in no degree interesting – to me who see nothing in England but the country which holds *you* – or around it but the sea which divides us. – They say absence destroys weak passions – & confirms strong ones – Alas! *mine* for you is the union of all passions & of all affections – Has strengthened itself but will destroy me

– I do not speak of *physical* destruction – for I have endured & can endure much – but of the annihilation of all thoughts feelings or hopes – which have not more or less a reference to you & to *our recollections.*

Ever dearest

Simone de Beauvoir to Jean-Paul Sartre
Wednesday [27 July 1938]

Hôtel de la gare, Albertville (Savoie)

Dear little being,

I'm not going to write you a long letter, though I've hundreds of things to tell you, because I prefer to tell them in person on Saturday. You should know, however:

1. First, that I love you dearly – I'm quite overcome at the thought that I'll see you disembarking from the train on Saturday, carrying your suitcase and my red hatbox – I can already picture us ensconced on our deckchairs overlooking a lovely blue sea and talking nineteen to the dozen – and I feel a great sense of well-being.

2. You've been very sweet to write me such long letters. I'm hoping for another this evening at Annecy. You tell me countless pleasing little items of news, but

the most pleasing of all is that you've found your subject. The big page looks extremely fine with that title, just the perverse kind you like: *Lucifer* – I can find no fault with it.

3. Something extremely agreeable has happened to me, which I didn't at all expect when I left – I slept with Little Bost three days ago. It was I who propositioned him, of course. Both of us had been wanting it: we'd have serious conversations during the day, and the evenings would be unbearably oppressive. One rainy evening at Tignes, in a barn, lying face down a few inches away from one another, we gazed at each other for an hour finding various pretexts to put off the moment of going to sleep, he babbling frantically, I racking my brains vainly for the casual, appropriate words I couldn't manage to articulate – I'll tell you it all properly later. In the end I laughed foolishly and looked at him, so he said: 'Why are you laughing?' and I said: 'I'm trying to picture your face if I propositioned you to sleep with me' and he said: 'I was thinking that you were thinking that I wanted to kiss you but didn't dare.' After that we floundered on for another quarter of an hour before he made up his mind to kiss me. He was tremendously astonished when I told him I'd always had a soft spot for him – and he ended up telling me yesterday evening that he'd loved me for ages. I'm very fond of him. We spend idyllic days, and nights of passion. But have no

fear of finding me sullen or disoriented or ill at ease on Saturday; it's something precious to me, something intense, but also light and easy and properly in its place in my life, simply a happy blossoming of relations that I'd always found very agreeable. It strikes me as funny, on the other hand, to think that I'm now going to spend two days with Védrine.

Goodbye, dear little being – I'll be on the platform on Saturday, or at the buffet if you don't see me on the platform. I'd like to spend long weeks alone with you. A big kiss.

Your Beaver

William Congreve to Arabella Hunt

Dear Madam,

May I presume to beg pardon for the fault I committed. So foolish a fault that it was below not only a man of sense but a man; and of which nothing could ever have made me guilty but the fury of a passion with which none but your lovely self could inspire me. May I presume to beg pardon for a fault which I can never forgive myself? To purchase that pardon what would I not endure? You shall see me prostrate before you, and use me like a slave while I kiss the dear feet that trample upon me. But if my crime be too great for forgiveness, as indeed it is very great, deny me not one dear parting look, let me see you once before I must never see you more.

Christ! I want patience to support that accursed thought, I have nothing in the world that is dear to me but you. You have made everything else indifferent; and can I resolve never to see you more? In spight of myself I must always see you. Your form is fixed by fate in my mind and is never to be remov'd. I see those lovely piercing eyes continually, I see each moment those ravishing lips which I have gazed on still with desire, and still have touch'd with transport, and at which I have so often flown with all the fury of the most violent love.

Jesus! from whence and whither am I fallen? From the hopes of blissful extasies to black despair! From the expectation of immortal transports, which none but your dear self can give me, and which none but he who loves like me could ever so much as think of, to a complication of cruel passions and the most dreadful condition of human life.

My fault indeed has been very great, and cries aloud for the severest vengeance. See it inflicted on me: see me despair and die for that fault. But let me not die unpardon'd, madam; I die for you, but die in the most cruel and dreadful manner. The wretch that lies broken on the wheel alive feels not a quarter of what I endure.

Yet boundless love has been all my crime; unjust, ungrateful, barbarous return for it!

Suffer me to take my eternal leave of you; when I have done that how easy will it be to bid all the rest of the world adieu.

ABOUT LETTERS

Elizabeth Linley to R. B. Sheridan   11 o'clock

Though I parted from you so lately, and though I expect to see you again so soon, yet I cannot keep my fingers from the pen but I must be plaguing you with my scrawl. Oh, my dearest love, I am never happy but when I am with you. I cannot speak or think of anything else. When shall we have another happy half hour? I declare I have not felt real joy since I came from France before this evening. Perhaps now while I am writing and amusing myself by expressing the tender sentiments which I feel for you, you are flirting with Miss W, or some other handsome girl ...

I really think Charles suspected something this evening. He looked amazingly knowing this evening when I came down. Deuce take his curious head. I wish he would mind his own business and not interrupt us in our stolen pleasures. Is it not amazing, my dear Love, that we should always have so great an inclination for what is not in our possession? ...

Let me see, what have I more to say? – nothing but the same dull story over and over again – that I love you to distraction, and that I would prefer you and beggary before any other man and a throne. I will call you Horatio – that was the name you gave yourself in that sweet poem – write to me then, my dear Horatio, and tell me that you are equally sincere and constant ...

My hand shakes so at this moment I can scarce hold the pen. My father came into my room this moment, and I had just time to stuff the letter behind the glass. 'Twas well he did not take much notice of me, for I was ... Goodbye. God bless – I will ...

Katherine Mansfield to John Middleton Murry
Saturday night, 18 May 1917

24 Redcliffe Road, Fulham

My darling

Do not imagine, because you find these lines in your private book that I have been trespassing. You know I have not – and where else shall I leave a love letter? For I long to write you a love letter tonight. You are all about me – I seem to breathe you – hear you – feel you in me and of me – What am I doing here? You are away – I have seen you in the train, at the station, driving up, sitting in the lamplight talking, greeting people – washing your hands – And I am here – in your tent – sitting at your table. There are some wallflower petals on the table and a dead match, a blue pencil and a Magdeburgische Zeitung. I am just as much at home as they.

When dusk came – flowing up the silent garden – lapping against the blind windows – my first & last terror started up – I was making some coffee in the kitchen. It was so violent so dreadful I put down the coffee-pot – and simply ran away – ran out of the studio and up the street with my bag under one arm and a block of writing paper and a pen under the other. I felt that if I could get here & find Mrs [illegible] I should be 'safe' – I found her and I lighted your gas, wound up your clock – drew your curtains – & embraced your black overcoat before I sat down – frightened no longer. Do not be angry with me, Bogey – ca a ete plus fort que moi . . . That is why I am here.

When you came to tea this afternoon you took a brioche broke it in half & padded the inside doughy bit with two fingers. You always do that with a bun or a roll or a piece of bread – It is your way – your head a little on one side the while . . .

– When you opened your suitcase I saw your old feltie and a French book and a comb all higgledy piggledy – 'Tig. I've only got 3 handkerchiefs' – Why should that memory be so sweet to me? . . .

Last night, there was a moment before you got into bed. You stood, quite naked, bending forward a little – talking. It was only for an instant. I saw you – I loved you so – loved your body with such tenderness – Ah my dear – And I am not thinking now of 'passion'. No, of that other thing that makes me feel that every inch of you is so precious to me. Your soft shoulders – your creamy warm skin, your ears, cold like shells are cold – your long legs and your feet that I love to clasp with my feet – the feeling of your belly – & your thin young back – Just below that bone that sticks out at the back of your neck you have a little mole. It is partly because we are young that I feel this tenderness – I love your youth – I could not bear that it should be touched even by a cold wind if I were the Lord.

We two, you know have everything before us, and we shall do very great things – I have perfect faith in us – and so perfect is my love for you that I am, as it were, still, silent to my very soul. I want nobody but you for my lover and my friend and to nobody but you shall I be *faithful.*

I am yours for ever.

Tig

Leŏs Janáček to Kamila Stosslova
Brno, 1 February 1928, at night

My dear Kamila!

I came to my post box, saw your letter lying there – and gasped with joy! I am now writing before opening your letter. I know that without you my life would be a parched meadow. At each step I would say, there a flower once blossomed, here another – and there would be sadness to choking point. Now I shall read your letter! I think that it will give me pleasure – if only because you have written! I have read both letters – and I am immensely pleased to recognize my Kamila again! No, Kamilka, do write. Even if you only write, I am fine, I think about it with happiness – it will revive me as well as you.

I am glad that you have forgiven me. My letters, I know, have turned bitter. Now it will be different.

I have now begun to write something nice. Our life will be in it. It'll be called 'Love letters'.

I think it's going to sound delightful. After all, those pleasant experiences of ours have already been plentiful enough! Like little fires in my soul, they will light up into the most beautiful melodies.

Just imagine! I finished the first movement in Hukvaldy. That impression on seeing you for the first time!

Now I am working on the second movement; I think it will dawn on that hot [word scratched out in original letter] in Luhačovice. In particular, the whole work will be held together by a special instrument. It's called the *viola d'amour* – the viola of love. Oh, how I am looking forward to it! In this work I shall always be alone with you! No third person beside us. Full of longings as if with you there in that heaven of ours. How I shall enjoy working on it. After all, you must know that, apart from you, I know no other world! You are everything to me, I want nothing else but your love.

And how bitter I was when I read in your letter how you would like to forget everything beautiful that has passed between us! I was thinking, is it possible that my Kamila can forget it all? Could it be possible? Now I know that it couldn't! In our heaven we have reached that point where it's no longer possible to go back, only upwards! Draw strength from this; you are certain to find peace. If I am somebody and my works count, then it follows that you are also somebody – and higher and more important than that ordinary niece of mine, who will never be allowed to stand in my presence again. That's how it is, my dear Kamilka! Don't blame your nerves for everything; that bronchitis has put you into a terrible mood. It'll also pass.

And don't be ashamed of your nature. It's so dear, so very dear to me. You are laughter 'mixed' from tears. It is that nature – I understand it quite a lot already – which is almost chronically sensitive. You are difficult to understand. What surrounds you is hard – and, Kamilka, heartless. It's better to avoid hard stones than to fall among them.

So, my precious Kamilka, keep writing; if it's only two or three words it'll satisfy me.

And were you to write 'I am forever yours', you would open heaven for me! . . .

Forever yours

L

Mary Wollstonecraft to Gilbert Imlay
Paris, 1793, Friday morning

I am glad to find that other people can be unreasonable as well as myself; for be it known to thee that I answered thy *first* letter the very night it reached me (Sunday), though thou couldst not receive it before Wednesday, because it was not sent off till the next day. There is a full, true, and particular account.

Yet I am not angry with thee, my love, for I think that it is a proof of stupidity, and likewise of a milk-and-water affection, which comes to the same thing when the temper is governed by a square and compass. There is nothing picturesque in this straight-lined equality, and the passions always give grace to the actions.

Recollection now makes my heart bound to thee; but it is not to thy money-getting face, though I cannot be seriously displeased with the exertion which increases my esteem, or rather is what I should have expected from thy character. No; I have thy honest countenance before me – relaxed by tenderness; a little – little wounded by my whims; and thy eyes glittering with sympathy. Thy lips then feel softer than soft, and I rest my cheek on thine, forgetting all the world. I have not left the hue of love out of the picture – the rosy glow; and fancy has spread it over my own cheeks, I believe, for I feel them burning, whilst a delicious tear trembles in my eye that would be all your own, if a grateful emotion directed to the Father of nature, who has made me thus alive to happiness, did not give more warmth to the sentiment it divides. I must pause a moment.

Need I tell you that I am tranquil after writing thus? I do not know why, but I have more confidence in your affection, when absent, than present; nay, I think that you must love me, for, in the sincerity of my heart let me say it, I believe I deserve your tenderness, because I am true, and have a degree of sensibility that you can see and relish.

Yours sincerely,

Mary

George Farquhar to Anne Oldfield   *[1699?]*

Madam,

If I haven't begun thrice to write and as often thrown away my pen, may I never take it up again; my head and my heart have been at cuffs about you two long hours, –

says my head, you're a coxcomb for troubling your noddle with a lady whose beauty is as much above your pretensions as your merit is below her love.

Then answers my heart, – Good Mr Head, you're a blockhead. I know Mr F—r's merit better than you; as for your part, I know you to be as whimsical as the devil, and changing with every new notion that offers, but for my share I am fixt, and can stick to my opinion of a lady's merit for ever, and if the fair she can secure an interest in me, Monsieur Head, you may go whistle.

Come, come, (answered my head) you, Mr Heart, are always leading the gentleman into some inconvenience or other; was it not you that first enticed him to talk to this lady? Your damn'd confounded warmth made him like this lady, and your busy impertinence has made him write to her; your leaping and skipping disturbs his sleep by night and his good humour by day; in short, sir, I will hear no more on't; I am head, and will be obeyed.

You lie, sir, replied my heart (being very angry), I am head in matters of love, and if you don't give your consent, you shall be forced, for I am sure that in this case all the members will be on my side. What say you, gentlemen Hands!

Oh (say the hands), we would not forego the tickling pleasure of touching a delicious white soft skin for the world.

Well, what say you, Mr Tongue?

Zounds, says the linguist, there is more extasy in speaking three soft words of Mr Heart's suggesting than whole orations of Signior Head's, so I am for the lady, and here's my honest neighbour, Lips, will stick to't.

By the sweet power of kisses, that we will, (replied the lips) and presently some other worthy members, standing up for the Heart, they laid violent hands (*nemine contradicente*) on poor Head, and knocked out his brains. So now, madam, behold me, as perfect a lover as any in Christendom, my heart firmly dictating every word I say. The little rebel throws itself into your power, and if you don't support it in the cause it has taken up for your sake, think what will be the condition of the headless and heartless

Farquhar

Dorothy Osborne to Sir William Temple [*6 March 1653?*]

Sir,

Your last letter came like a pardon to one upon the block. I have given over the hopes on't, having received my letters by the other carrier, who uses always to be last. The loss put me hugely out of order, and you would both have pitied and laughed at me if you could have seen how woodenly I entertained the widow, who came hither the day before, and surprised me very much. Not being able to say anything, I got her to cards, and there with a great deal of patience lost my money to her – or rather I gave it as my ransom. In the midst of our play, in comes my blessed boy with your letter, and, in earnest, I was not able to disguise the joy it gave me, though one was by that is not much your friend, and took notice of a blush that for my life I could not keep back. I put up the letter in my pocket, and made what haste I could to lose the money I had left, that I might take occasion to go fetch some more; but I did not make such haste back again, I can assure you. I took time enough to have coined myself some money if I had had the art on't, and left my brother enough to make all his addresses to her if he were so disposed. I know not whether he was pleased or not, but I am sure I was ...

Oscar Wilde to Constance Wilde
The Balmoral, Edinburgh, Tuesday, 16 December 1884

Dear and Beloved,

Here am I, and you at the Antipodes. O execrable facts, that keep our lips from kissing, though our souls are one.

What can I tell you by letter? Alas! nothing that I would tell you. The messages of the gods to each other

201

travel not by pen and ink and indeed your bodily presence here would not make you more real: for I feel your fingers in my hair, and your cheek brushing mine. The air is full of the music of your voice, my soul and body seem no longer mine, but mingled in some exquisite ecstasy with yours. I feel incomplete without you.

Ever and ever yours

Oscar

Here I stay till Sunday.

Alban Berg to Helene Nahowski   Berghof, 18 July 1908

'When someone writes a letter to a very good friend, or even more, to his beloved, he puts on his best attire, as well he may. For in the quiet of his letter, on the tranquil blue paper, he can express his truest feelings. The tongue and the spoken word have become so soiled by their every-day use, they cannot speak out loud the beauty which the pen can quietly write.'

I couldn't help thinking of that passage from Strindberg when I got your letter this morning ...

My longing for the mountains is roused again by the lovely little flowers you sent. How lucky you are! Only in my dreams can I gaze on the mountain meadows, with their mauve forget-me-nots and black bugles and fiery red rhododendrons, and the precipices with their scattered tree-stumps and branches, and the black salamanders in the white boulders, and flocks of grouse under stunted dwarf-pines. All that is your realm, in which you are queen. And we who live in the plains can only look fondly up at those heights in envy or admiration.

Yet I know the paths which lead up there, the less frequented paths too. And somewhere far above, amidst the clouds and winds, I shall be waiting for you, my hand outstretched in greeting – cold as ice yet warm with life in its love.

And woe betide anyone else who crosses my path whistling Wagner! I'll soon strike his top note off his shoulders!

But now out of my best attire (which looks a bit like tourist dress) and into every-day clothes, for the postman waits! More from Strindberg, though, to end up with: 'It is no pose or deceit if lovers' souls should show up better in their letters to each other than in real life. Nor is the lover false in his love letters. He is not making himself out better than he is: he is *becoming* better, and in these moments *is* better. He is truly himself in such moments, the greatest moments life can bestow on us.'

All yours

Alban

Virginia Woolf to Vita Sackville-West
Sunday [7 October]

52 Tavistock Square

Dearest Creature,

It was a very very nice letter you wrote by the light of the stars at midnight. Always write then, for your heart requires moonlight to deliquesce it. And mine is fried in gaslight, as it is only nine o'clock and I must go to bed at eleven. And so I shant say anything: not a word of the balm to my anguish – for I am always anguished – that you were to me. How I watched you! How I felt – now what was it like? Well, somewhere I have seen a little ball kept bubbling up and down on the spray of a fountain: the fountain is you; the ball me. It is a sensation I get only from you. It is physically stimulating, restful at the same time . . .

Berg

Michael Faraday to Sarah Barnard
Royal Institution, Thursday evening [December 1820]

My Dear Sarah,

It is astonishing how much the state of the body influences the powers of the mind. I have been thinking all the morning of the very delightful and interesting letter I would send you this evening, and now I am so tired, and yet have so much to do, that my thoughts are quite giddy, and run round your image without any power of themselves to stop and admire it. I want to say a thousand kind and, believe me, heartfelt things to you, but am not master of words fit for the purpose; and still, as I ponder and think on you, chlorides, trials, oil, Davy, steel, miscellanea, mercury, and fifty other professional fancies swim before and drive me further and further into the quandary of stupidness.

From your affectionate

Michael

Stella Campbell to Bernard Shaw   8 April 1913

33 Kensington Square, W

I really wrote you a delicious letter 3 days ago but when I came to look it over barely one word was legible. I thought only the greatest love in the world could make excuses for such unseemly unsightly ~~penmanship~~ scrawlsmanship – as a matter of fact one tiny word in your supplementary letter sent me astray . . .

Here am I writing in my bed in Kensington Square once more!

If those young lions could hear what I have heard their heads would be bowed in worship, their hands raised in prayer – the angels sing at sweet visionings the song my singing bird sang to me.

I send you one of your letters to read that somehow has missed the waste paper basket . . .

Yes I think Barrie will be faithful if I can *wait*. What will you be I wonder –

My love to you

Stella

Esther Van Homrigh (Vanessa) to Jonathan Swift
London, 1 September 1712

Had I a correspondent in China, I might have had an answer by this time. I never could think till now that London was so far off in your thoughts and that twenty miles were by your computation equal to some thousands. I thought it a piece of charity to undeceive you in this point and to let you know, if you'll give yourself the trouble to write, I may probably receive your letter in a day. 'Twas that made me venture to take pen in hand the third time. Sure you'll not let it be to no purpose. You must needs be extremely happy where you are, to forget your absent friends; and I believe you have formed a new system and think there is no more of this world, passing your sensible horizon. If this be your notion I must excuse you; if not, you can plead no other excuse; and if it be so, I must reckon myself of another world; but I shall have much ado to be persuaded till you send me some convincing arguments of it. Don't dally in a thing of this consequence, but demonstrate that 'tis possible to keep up a correspondence between friends, though in different worlds, and assure one another, as I do you, that

    I am

        Your most obedient & humble servant

                E. Van Homrigh

Napoleon Bonaparte to Josephine Bonaparte
Verona, 3 Frimaire, year V [1797]

To Josephine, in Milan

    I love you no longer; on the contrary, I detest you. You are a wretch, truly perverse, truly stupid, a real Cinderella. You never write to me at all, you do not love your husband; you know the pleasure that your letters give him yet you cannot even manage to write him half a dozen lines, thrown off in a moment!

    What then do you do all day, Madame? What business is so vital that it robs you of the time to write to your faithful lover? What attachment can be stifling and pushing aside the love, the tender and constant love which you promised him? Who can this wonderful new lover be who takes up your every moment, rules your days and prevents you from devoting your attention to your husband? Beware, Josephine; one fine night the doors will be broken down and there I shall be.

In truth, I am worried, my love, to have no news from you; write me a four-page letter at once made up from those delightful words which fill my heart with emotion and joy.

I hope to hold you in my arms before long, when I shall lavish upon you a million kisses, burning as the equatorial sun.

Bonaparte

Franz Kafka to Felice Bauer   *13 October 1912*

Pořič 7, Prague

Dear Fräulein Bauer,

Fifteen days ago, at ten o'clock in the morning, I received your first letter, and a few minutes later I sat down and wrote you four pages of enormous size. I don't regret it, for I could not have spent the time with greater pleasure, and my only regret is that when I had finished I had made but a very small beginning of what I wanted to say, so that the suppressed part of the letter preoccupied me for days and made me restless, until this restlessness was replaced by the anticipation of your reply and the gradual waning of this anticipation.

But why haven't you written to me? – It is possible, and from the manner of that letter even probable, that there was something foolish in it that may have disconcerted you, but it is not possible that the good intention behind my every word could have escaped you. – Could a letter have gone astray? But mine was sent with too great an eagerness for it to have missed its aim, while yours was too eagerly awaited. And do letters really get lost except in the mind of one waiting for them and unable to find another explanation? – Could my letter possibly have been kept from you because of the frowned-upon trip to Palestine? But can this really happen within a family, and to you of all people? And according to my calculations the letter should have arrived on Sunday morning. – So there remains only the sad possibility that you are ill. But this I do not believe. Surely, you are healthy and cheerful. – But then my reason fails me, and I write this letter not so much in the hope of a reply as to discharge a duty towards myself.

If I were the Immanuelkirchstrasse postman delivering this letter to your house, I wouldn't allow myself to be detained by an astonished member of your family, but would walk straight through all the rooms to yours, and put the letter in your hands; or, better still, I would stand outside your door and keep on ringing the bell for my pleasure, a pleasure that would relieve all tension!

Yours,

Franz K

Alexander Pope to Teresa Blount   7 August 1716

Madam,

I have so much Esteem for you, and so much of the other thing, that were I a handsome fellow I should do you a vast deal of good: but as it is, all I am good for is to write a civil letter, or to make a fine Speech. The truth is, that considering how often & how openly I have declared Love to you, I am astonished (and a little affronted) that you have not forbid my correspondence, & directly said, *See my face no more.* It is not enough, Madam, for your reputation that you keep your hands pure, from the Stain of Such Ink as might be shed to gratify a male Correspondent; Alas! while your heart consents to encourage him in this lewd liberty of writing, you are not (indeed you are not) what you would so fain have me think you, a Prude! I am vain enough to conclude (like most young fellows) that a fine Lady's Silence is Consent, and so I write on.

But in order to be as Innocent as possible in this Epistle, I'll tell you news. You have asked me News a thousand times at the first word you spoke to me, which some would interpret as if you expected nothing better from my lips: And truly 'tis not a sign Two Lovers are together, when they can be so impertinent as to enquire what the World does? All I mean by this is, that either you or I cannot be in love with the other; I leave you to guess which of the two is that stupid & insensible Creature, so blind to the others Excellencies and Charms . . .

WARNING

Zelda Fitzgerald to F. Scott Fitzgerald [*c. 1919*]

Scott, you're really awful silly – In the first place, I haven't kissed anybody good-bye, and in the second place, nobody's left in the first place – You know, darling, that I love you too much to want to. If I did have an honest – or dishonest – desire to kiss just one or two people, I *might* – but I couldn't ever want to – my mouth is yours.

But s'pose I did – Don't you know it'd just be absolutely *nothing* – Why can't you understand that nothing means anything except your darling self and your love – I wish we'd hurry and I'd be yours so you'd *know* – Sometimes I almost despair of making you feel sure – so sure that nothing could ever make you doubt like I do –

Bernard Shaw to Stella Campbell   *8 November 1912*

10 Adelphi Terrace, WC

Stella, Stella

Shut your ears tight against this blarneying Irish liar and actor. Read no more of his letters. He will fill his fountain pen with your heart's blood, and sell your most sacred emotions on the stage. He is a mass of imagination with no heart. He is a writing and talking machine that has worked for nearly forty years until its skill is devilish. I should have warned you before; but I thought his white hairs and 56 years had made his philanderings ridiculous, and that you would beat him at his own game and revenge his earlier victims. I pray still that you, great actress as you are, are playing with him as he is playing with you. He cares for nothing really but his mission, as he calls it, and his work. He is treacherous as only an Irishman can be: he adores you with one eye and sees you with the other as a calculated utility. He has been recklessly trying to please you, to delight you, to persuade you to carry him up to heaven for a moment (he is trying to do it *now*); and when you have done it, he will run away and give it all to the mob. All his goods are in the shop window; and he'll steal *your* goods and put them there too.

But don't cut him off utterly. He is really worth something, even to *you*, if you harden your heart against him. He will tell you that you are too great a woman to belong to any man, meaning, I suppose that he is too great a man to belong to any woman. He will warn you against himself with passionate regard for you – sincerely too, and yet knowing it to be one of his most dangerous tricks. He will warn you against his warning you, not meaning you to take any warning; and he will say later on 'I told you so'. His notion of a woman in love with him is one who turns white and miserable when he comes into the room, and is all one wretched jealous reproach. Oh dont, dont, DONT fall in love with him; but dont grudge him the joy he finds in being in love with you, and writing all sorts of wild but heartfelt exquisite lies – lies, lies, lies, lies to you, his adoredest.

G.B.S.

Esther Van Homrigh to Jonathan Swift   *Dublin, 1720*

Is it possible that again you will do the very same thing I warned you of so lately? I believe you thought I only rallied when I told you, the other night, I would pester you with letters. Did not I know you very well, I should think you knew but little of the world, to imagine that a woman would not keep her word whenever she promised anything that was malicious. Had not you better a thousand times throw away one hour, at some time or other of the day, than to be interrupted in your business at this rate? For I know 'tis as impossible for you to burn my letters without reading them, as 'tis for me to avoid reproving you when you behave yourself so wrong. Once more I advise you, if you have any regard for your quiet, to alter your behaviour quickly; for I do assure you I have too much spirit to sit contented with this treatment. Now, because I love frankness extremely, I here tell you that I have determined to try all manner of human arts to reclaim you, and if all those fail, I am resolved to have recourse to the black one, which it is said, never does. Now see what inconveniences you will bring both me and yourself into. Pray think calmly of it. Is it not much better to come of yourself than to be brought by force, and that, perhaps, at a time when you have the most agreeable engagement in the world? For when I undertake anything, I don't love to do it by halves. But there is one thing that falls out very luckily for you, which is that, of all the passions, revenge hurries me least, so that you have it yet in your power to turn all this fury into good humour, and, depend upon it, and more I assure you. Come at what time you please, you can never fail of being very well received.

Esther Van Homrigh to Jonathan Swift   Dublin, 1714

Well, now I plainly see how great a regard you have for me. You bid me be easy, and you'd see me as often as you could. You had better said, as often as you could get the better of your inclinations so much, or as often as you remembered there was such a one in the world. If you continue to treat me as you do you will not be made uneasy by me long. 'Tis impossible to describe what I have suffered since I saw you last; I am sure I could have bore the rack much better than those killing, killing words of yours. Sometimes I have resolved to die without seeing you more; but those resolves, to your misfortune, did not last long. For there is something in human nature that prompts one so to find relief in this world, I must give way to it, and beg you'd see me and speak kindly to me; for I am sure you'd not condemn anyone to suffer what I have done, could you but know it. The reason I write to you is because I cannot tell i[t] you, should I see you; for when I begin to complain, then you are angry, and there is something in your look so awful, that it strikes me dumb. Oh! that you may but have so much regard for me left, that this complaint may touch your soul with pity. I say as little as ever I can: did you but know what I thought, I am sure it would move you. Forgive me, and believe I cannot help telling you this, and live.

Lord Nelson to Lady Hamilton   17 February 1801

I am so agitated that I can write nothing. I knew it would be so, and you can't help it. Why did you not tell Sir William? Your character will be gone. Good God! he will be next you, and telling you soft things. If he does, tell it out at table, and turn him out of the house. Do not sit long. If you sing a song, I know you cannot help it, do not let him set next you, but at dinner he will hob glasses with you. I cannot write to Sir Wm, but he ought to go to the Prince and not suffer your character to be ruined by him. O, God, that I was dead! But I do not, my dearest Emma, blame you, nor do I fear your inconstancy. I tremble, and God knows how I write. Can nothing be thought of? I am gone almost mad, but you cannot help it. It will be in all the newspapers with hints. Recollect what the villain said to Mr Nisbet, *how you hit his fancy.* I am mad, almost dead, but ever for ever yours to the last moment, your, only your, &c.

I could not write another line if I was to be made King. If I was in town nothing should make me dine with you that damned day, but, my dear Emma, I do not blame you, only remember your poor miserable friend, that you must be singing and appear gay. I shall that day have no one to dinner; it shall be a fast day to me. He will put his foot near you. I pity you from my soul, as I feel confident you wish him in hell. Have plenty of people and do not say a word you can help to him. He wishes, I dare say, to have you alone. Don't let him touch, nor yet sit next you; if he comes, get up. God strike him blind if he looks at you – this is high treason, and you may get me hanged by revealing it. Oh, God! that I were. I have read your letter, your resolution never to go where the fellow is, but you must have him at home. Oh, God! but you cannot, I suppose, help it, and you cannot turn him out of your own house. He will stay and sup and sit up till 4 in the morning, and the fewer that stay the better. Oh, God! why do I live? But I do not blame you; it is my misfortune. I feel nobody uses me ill. I am only fit to be second, or third, or 4, or to black shoes. I want no better part than I have. I see your determination to be on your guard, and am as fixed as fate. If you'll believe me, don't scold me; I am more dead than alive, to the last breath yours. If you cannot get rid of this I hope you will tell Sir William never to bring the fellow again.

I send a note for Mrs T.

Mozart to his wife   Vienna, middle of August 1789

Dearest little Wife!

I was delighted to get your dear letter – and I trust that you received yesterday my second one together with the infusion, the electuaries and the ants' eggs. I shall sail off to you at five o'clock to-morrow morning. Were it not for the joy of seeing you again and embracing you, I should not drive out to Baden just yet, for 'Figaro' is going to be performed very soon, and as I have some alterations to make, my presence will be required at the rehearsals. I shall probably have to be back here by the 19th. But to stay here until the 19th without you would be quite impossible. Dear little wife! I want to talk to you quite frankly. You have no reason whatever to be unhappy. You have a husband who loves you and does all he possibly can for you. As for your foot, you must just be patient and it will surely get well again. I am glad indeed when you have some fun – of course I am – but I do wish that you would not sometimes make yourself so cheap. In my opinion you are too free and easy with [name deleted] and it was the same with [name deleted], when he was still at Baden. Now please remember that [name deleted] are not half so familiar with other women, whom they perhaps know more intimately, as they are with you. Why, [name deleted] who is usually a well-conducted fellow and particularly respectful to women, must have been misled by your behaviour into writing the most disgusting and most impertinent *sottises* which he put into his letter. A woman must always make herself respected, or else people will begin to talk about her. My love! Forgive me for being so frank, but my peace of mind demands it as well as our mutual happiness. Remember that you yourself once admitted to me that you were inclined to comply too easily. You know the consequences of that. Remember too the promise you gave to me. Oh, God, do try, my love! Be merry and happy and charming to me. Do not torment yourself and me with unnecessary jealousy. Believe in my love, for surely you have proofs of it, and you will see how happy we shall be. Rest assured that it is only by her prudent behaviour that a wife can enchain her husband. Adieu. To-morrow I shall kiss you most tenderly.

Mozart

Alexander Pushkin to Natalia Pushkin   Boldino,
30 October 1833

Yesterday I received both your letters, dear heart; I thank you. But I must read the Riot Act to you a little. You seem only to think now of flirting – but look here; it is not the fashion any more and is considered as the mark of bad bringing-up. There is little sense in it. You are pleased that men run after you – much cause for pleasure! Not only you, but Praskowja Petrowna could succeed with ease in getting all the unmarried pack of loafers to run after her. When the trough is there, the pigs come of their own accord. Why do you need to receive men who make love to you in your house? One can never know what sort of people one may come across. Read the Ismailov fable of Foma and Kusma. Foma entertains Kusma with caviar and herring.

Kusma wished to drink after that. But Foma gave him nothing; whereupon the guest gave the host a sound thrashing. From this the poet draws the moral lesson; You pretty women! do not give your adorers a herring to eat, if you have no intention of giving them something to drink afterwards; for you could easily come across a Kusma. Do you see? I beg of you, to arrange no academical dinners in my house...

And now, my angel, I kiss you, as if nothing had happened, and thank you, that you have elaborately and sincerely described your entire life of pleasure. Have a good time, little wife, but do not overdo it and do not forget me altogether. I can hardly hold out any longer – so keen am I to see you *coiffée à la Ninon*; you must look delicious. Why did you not think before of this old strumpet and copy her coiffure? Write to me, what successes you have at balls ... And my angel, please, please, do not flirt too outrageously. I am not jealous, and I know that you will not overstep the utmost limits, but you know how I dislike everything which smells of our Moscow 'young ladies', who do not surpass the *il faut*, who are what one calls in English 'vulgar'... If I find on my return, that your dear, simple aristocratic tone has changed, I shall get a divorce, I swear to you, and become a soldier out of grief. You ask me, how I do, and whether I have become handsomer. To begin with, I am growing a beard, whiskers, and moustache which are an ornament to man; when I go out into the street, they call me uncle; secondly, I wake up at 7 o'clock, drink coffee, and lie in bed till 3 o'clock. Lately I started writing, and have scribbled a lot of stuff; at 3 o'clock I go riding, at 5 I take a bath, and then comes my dinner – potatoes and buckwheat. Till 9 o'clock I read. Thus the day passes, and every day is alike.

Evelyn Waugh to Laura Waugh   7 January 1945

37 Military Mission [Dubrovnik]

Darling Laura, sweet whiskers, do try to write me better letters. Your last, dated 19 December received today, so eagerly expected, was a bitter disappointment. Do realize that a letter need not be a bald chronicle of events; I know you lead a dull life now, my heart bleeds for it, though I believe you could make it more interesting if you had the will. But that is no reason to make your letters as dull as your life. I simply am not interested in Bridget's children. Do grasp that. A letter should be a form of conversation; write as though you were talking to me.

For instance you say my Christmas presents have arrived and Eddie [Grant] is pleased. What do you think of the book? Your copy is still binding but you must have seen his. You know I have not seen one. Tell me what it is like. It is dedicated to you. Are you pleased to see it in this form? Are you curious to know what changes I have made in the final proofs? There are many changes in this copy from what you read before. Can you not see how it disappoints me that this book which I regard as my first important one, and have dedicated to you, should have no comment except that Eddie is pleased with it.

Has no wine come for you? I ordered some. Perhaps there is none left in London.

No Christmas presents came from you to me.

Today is the Orthodox Christmas. I have just been to a 'tea party' to which I was invited at 3 p.m. With savage peoples one knows so little what to expect, so after a heavy luncheon I set out and was given a place at a table already full. First I was given green chartreuse and ham, then tea and cakes then cherry brandy and cigarettes. It seemed the end but suddenly a whole cold roast sheep was brought in; there were red wine & speeches until 6.30 p.m.

Do write & tell me what you are thinking & how you are looking. Be natural when you write. Don't send any more of these catalogues of family facts. Tell me what letters of mine you have had.

Evelyn

I have passed the last 40 years of my life in the hurry &
bustle that must necessarily be attendant on a publick
character. I am arrived at the age when some repose is
really necessary, & I promised myself a quiet home, &
altho' I was sensible, & said so when I married, that I
shou'd be superannuated when my wife wou'd be in her
full beauty and vigour of youth. That time is arrived,
and we must make the best of it for the comfort of both
parties. Unfortunately our tastes as to the manner of
living are very different. I by no means wish to live in
solitary retreat, but to have seldom less than 12 or 14 at
table, & those varying continually, is coming back to
what was become so irksome to me in Italy during the
latter years of my residence in that country. I have no
connections out of my own family. I have no complaint
to make, but I feel that the whole attention of my wife is
given to Ld N. and his interest at Merton. I well know
the purity of Ld N.'s friendship for Emma and me, and I
know how very uncomfortable it wou'd make his Lp,
our best friend, if a separation shou'd take place, & am
therefore determined to do all in my power to prevent
such an extremity, which wou'd be *essentially detrimental*
to all parties, but wou'd be more sensibly felt by our
dear friend than by us. Provided that our expences in
housekeeping do not encrease beyond measure (of

which I must own I see some danger), I am willing to go on upon our present footing; but as I cannot expect to live many years, every moment to me is precious, & I hope I may be allow'd sometimes to be my own master, & pass my time according to my own inclination, either by going my fishing parties on the Thames or by going to London to attend the Museum, R. Society, the Tuesday Club, & Auctions of pictures. I mean to have a light chariot or post chaise by the month, that I may make use of it in London and run backwards and forwards to Merton or to Shepperton, &c. This is my plan, & we might go on very well, but I am fully determined not to have more of the very silly altercations that happen between us but too often and embitter the present moments exceedingly. If realy one cannot live comfortably together, a wise and well concerted separation is preferable; but I think, considering the probability of my not troubling any party long in this world, the best for us all wou'd be to bear those ills we have rather than flie to those we know not of. I have fairly stated what I have on my mind. There is not time for nonsense or trifling. I know and admire your talents & many excellent qualities, but I am not blind to your defects, & confess having many myself; therefore let us bear and forbear for God's sake.

Dear Princess Bibesco,

I am afraid you must stop writing these little love letters to my husband while he and I live together. It is one of the things which is not done in our world.

You are very young. Won't you ask your husband to explain to you the impossibility of such a situation.

Please do not make me have to write to you again. I do not like scolding people and I simply hate having to teach them manners.

Yours sincerely,

Katherine Mansfield

PARTING

Franz Kafka to Felice Bauer   20 November 1912

Dearest, what have I done that makes you torment me so? No letter again today, neither by the first mail nor the second. You do make me suffer! While one written word from you could make me happy! You've had enough of me; there is no other explanation, it's not surprising after all; what is incomprehensible, though, is that you don't write and tell me so. If I am to go on living at all, I cannot go on vainly waiting for news of you, as I have done these last few interminable days. But I no longer have any hope of hearing from you. I shall have to repeat specifically the farewell you bid me in silence. I should like to throw myself bodily on this letter, so that it cannot be mailed, but it must be mailed. I shall expect no further letters.

Franz

Lord Byron to Lady Byron   8 February 1816

All I can say seems useless – and all I could say – might be no less unavailing – yet I still cling to the wreck of my hopes – before they sink forever. – Were you then *never* happy with me? – did you never at any time or times express yourself so? – have no marks of affection – of the warmest *and* most reciprocal attachment passed between us? – or did in fact hardly a day go down without some such on one side and generally on both? – do not mistake me – [two lines crossed out] I have not denied my state of mind – but you know it's causes – & were those deviations from calmness never followed by acknowledgement & repentance? – was not the last which occurred more particularly so? – & had I not – had we not – the days before & on the day when we parted – every reason to believe that we loved each other – that we were to meet again – were not your letters kind? – had I not acknowledged to you all my faults & follies – & assured you that some had not – & would not be repeated? – I do not require these questions to be answered to me – but to your own heart. – The day before I received your father's letter – I had fixed a day for rejoining you – if I did not write lately – Augusta did – and as you had been my proxy in correspondence with her – so did I imagine – she might be the same for me to you. – Upon your letter to me – this day – I surely may remark - that it's expressions imply a treatment which I am incapable of inflicting – and you of imputing to me – if aware of their latitude – & the extent of the inferences to be drawn from them. – This is not just – but I have no reproaches – nor the wish to find cause for them. – Will you see me? – when & where you please – in whose presence you please: – the interview shall pledge you to nothing – & I will say

& do nothing to agitate either — it is torture to correspond thus — & there are things to be settled & said which cannot be written. — You say 'it is my disposition to deem what I *have worthless*' — did I deem *you* so? — did I ever so express myself to you — or of you — to others? — You are much changed within these twenty days or you would never have thus poisoned your own better feelings — and trampled upon mine.

ever yrs. most truly & affectionately

B

Sarah Bernhardt to Jean Mounet-Sully   January 1874

As far as I know, I have done nothing to justify such behaviour, I've told you distinctly that I do not love you any longer. I shook your hand and asked you to accept friendship in place of love. Why do you reproach me? Surely not for lack of frankness. I have been loyal: I have never deceived you; I have been yours completely. It is your fault that you have not known how to hold on to what is yours.

Besides, dear Jean, you must realize that I am not made for happiness. It is not my fault that I am constantly in search of new sensations, new emotions. That is how I shall be until my life is worn away. I am just as unsatisfied the morning after, as I am the night before. My heart demands more excitement than anyone can give it. My frail body is exhausted by the act of love. Never is it the love I dream of.

At this moment I am in a state of complete prostration. My life seems to have stopped. I feel neither joy nor sorrow. I wish you could forget me. What can I do? You must not be angry with me. I'm an incomplete person but a good one at heart. If I could prevent your suffering I would do so!!! But you demand my love, and it is you who have killed it!

I beg you, Jean, let us be friends.

Freya Stark to Stewart Perowne   Asolo, 19 March 1951

My darling,

Things are so sad and superficial between us that I have long been feeling that they cannot go on as they were and have only waited to write or speak because I could not bear you to think that any trivial cause, or want of affection, made me do it; and also because I hoped that you yourself might feel this thing so near your heart as to make you speak before I left.

I don't know whose the fault, anyway it doesn't matter. If it were just that the thing has failed, it would be simple. We are both independent, and we could separate and go back to where we were. I do care for you, but I have tried to take myself out of this account and to think of the whole thing without any bias as far as I can; one of these days I believe you will discover that you do care.

Let it be friendship meanwhile, and not just acquaintance. Half a dozen people around us tell me their hearts more intimately than you do. Better just to come and go as friends and that I will always be. There is nothing but true affection in my heart.

I have kept this for a day before sending, feeling perhaps that I might not send it at all, but there *must* be a truth between us, and it is the truth. Let it not make any difference to what we are to each other, such dear friends, and with true and safe affection, let it only take away what there was of pretence. I long for you to come here and you know it is your true home.

Love,

Freya

Dorothy Thompson to Sinclair Lewis   [*1942*]

I cannot recall that you ever asked me what I would like, even in the years that we lived together. But what I do not like is a divorce, and I am not going to get one. I know the divorce laws of Vermont, for at one time, I confess, I thought of getting a divorce. It was because of the brutally inconsiderate manner of your treatment of our relationship in your affair with Marcella, even going so far as to introduce her to Wells as his future 'stepmother'. That filled me with blind rage, and I thought I should spare myself any future insults of this kind. But the very basis of my relationship to you is that I cannot cherish any grudge or feel even normal resentment against you that endures, or that changes my feelings. 'This is the way he is,' is the only answer I can find ...

Hundreds of times, Hal, you made me promise that I would never leave you and never divorce you. I made the promise, because I meant it, and felt so, also. Why should I believe that you meant that and mean this, or that you did not know your own mind then and do know it now? I have never been able to repudiate our marriage, even to myself. Now you ask me to do it publicly. Such a step would be an unbearable self-violation ... In a curious way you are asking me to make something between us mutual again – to make common an aversion as once you besought me to make common a love. But I cannot. It is *not* common. The whole case would be an unmitigated fraud. It would not make me free. I shall live with you, in one sense, to the end of my life ... Don't you see, Hal, that you are asking *me* to banish *your* resentment? And you ask me, by attempting to blackmail me through the child, knowing how deeply

I wish him to have a father. But your relationship to Michael depends upon your feelings for Michael, and nothing *I* do will influence those feelings. Only what you do will influence them. Either you care for him, or you don't. My getting a divorce will not awaken a love in your heart for our child, if it is not there ... I still live every day in the crazy illusion that the door will open and you will come back – as though from Bermuda. I know with my merciless intellect that you will not come home, but there are realms outside intelligence and outside logic.

Elinor Wylie to Horace Wylie   20 May 1927

Dearest Horace,

A strange thing is going to happen to you, for that thing is going to come true which undoubtedly you once desired, & for which you will now not care a straw. I am going to admit to you that I wish with all my heart I had never left you. I don't want you to keep this letter, & I hope – & trust – that you will tell no one, but although the admission may afford us both a certain pain, it is founded upon such deep principles of truth & affection that I feel it should be made.

You must not tell this, because the knowledge of it would give pain to Bill, who is one of the best people who ever lived & with whom I expect to pass the remainder of my days. But you & I know that that remainder is not long, & the entire past – which is so much longer – makes me wish to tell you the truth.

I love you, Horace, with an unchanged love which is far more than friendship, & which will certainly persist until my death. It is impossible for me to tell your present sentiments towards me, but it can hardly be a matter for regret that your former devotion should have bred a devotion in me which nothing could destroy.

In Paris I was constantly reminded of you, & although even if we had been together we should have been no longer young, no longer, perhaps, lovers, nevertheless I wished we were together. In England the same thing is true – you are constantly in my thoughts, & remembered with an affection which is undoubtedly the strongest I shall ever feel.

It seems to me that our – shall we dignify it by the name of tragedy, or shall we call it failure? – our whatever it was was one of the war's cruel mishaps – as much so as my miscarriages or the loss of your money. I do not admire myself for having fallen in love with the idea of freedom, & poetry, & New York, & any individual among them: the misery of Washington, of anonymous letters, of this & that – your memory may supply the rest – spoiled what must always seem to me the happiest part of my life – my life with you. It was not your fault in any way, and mine only in my inability to stand the terrible alterations in that life which Washington made.

If we had stayed in England? You will say – impossible. If we had stayed in Bar Harbour? You will say I would have died – in some bad way. I doubt it, in both instances. But this is because I wish we had never parted.

Well, my dear, do not think I am divorcing Bill or something like that. He is the best boy imaginable. I suppose it is, in a way, devilish to write this. But I loved you first, I loved you more, I loved him afterwards, but now, that I love you both, I love you best. Surely you must, in some way, be glad to know this.

If you ever want me, I will come back to you openly. I have never cheated any one, you know. But I don't suppose you do want it, & I think it is much better as it is. Only – well, if you had been me, you would have written this letter from this little house in Chelsea. Answer it.

Your

Elinor

Queen Victoria to the King of the Belgians
Osborne, 20 December 1861

MY *own* DEAREST, KINDEST *FATHER*, – For as such have
I *ever* loved you! The poor fatherless baby of eight
months is now the utterly broken-hearted and crushed
widow of forty-two! My *life* as a *happy* one is *ended!* the
world is gone for *me!* If I *must live* on (and I will do
nothing to make me worse than I am), it is henceforth
for our poor fatherless children – for my unhappy
country, which has lost *all* in losing him – and in *only*
doing what I know and *feel* he would wish, for he *is* near
me – his spirit will guide and inspire me! But oh! to be
cut off in the prime of life – to see our pure, happy, quiet,
domestic life, which *alone* enabled me to bear my *much*
disliked position, CUT OFF at forty-two – when I *had*
hoped with such instinctive certainty that God never
would part us, and would let us grow old together
(though *he* always talked of the shortness of life) – is *too*
awful, too cruel! And yet it *must* be for *his* good, his
happiness! His purity was too great, his aspiration *too*
high for this poor, *miserable* world! His great soul is *now*
only enjoying *that* for which it *was* worthy! And I will *not*
envy him – only pray that *mine* may be perfected by it
and fit to be with him eternally, for which blessed
moment I earnestly long. Dearest, dearest Uncle, *how*
kind of you to come! It will be an unspeakable *comfort,*

and you *can do* much to tell people to do what they ought to do. As for my *own good, personal* servants – poor Phipps in particular – nothing can be more devoted, heartbroken as they are, and anxious only to live as *he* wished!

Good Alice has been and is wonderful.

The 26th will suit me perfectly. Ever your devoted, wretched Child,

Victoria R.

Elizabeth Bishop to Maria Osser   2 October 1967

The saddest thing for me now is that I have never heard a word from Mary [Morse] (or Lota's doctor as far as that goes, but to hell with *him*). I know Mary must be suffering horribly and I had hoped that she would at last forgive me but probably she never will. She never understood me at all, anyway – and now I am horribly afraid that she is blaming me – thinks I didn't take good care of Lota, etc ... I am telling you because it is making me so terribly unhappy, I have to tell someone who knows us. I am very dumb about some things – this last year Lota told me Mary never *had* liked me – and since I did and do like her, even if I got drunk and was frightfully rude that one time (after 15 years of mutual forbearance and politeness, however) – this is hard for me to understand. Mary is so intensely maternal – you know she used to drive all the way to Rio [from Samambaia] just to pack Lota's bags for her when we went traveling. She could never understand, I know, that although my feelings were very different, Lota and I were extremely happy together in our own different ways – in fact I had 12 or 13 of the happiest years of my life with her, until that park started to go bad and people behaved so badly – and that is more than most people ever have, I think. I curse myself for going to Seattle, too, of course – but at the time Lota did not object – in fact went with me to have new clothes made, and so on – it was only later when she began to get sick (before I got back, I think) that she began to think of my leaving as just one more betrayal. I never meant it that way, God knows, and was terribly homesick and almost came home in midterm – but she would never believe any of this. I also bored total strangers with stories of the [Flamingo] park and photographs – and poor Lota finally thought I wasn't interested in it, or proud of her! However – those ideas seemed to have cleared up, from her letters – and she certainly said nothing about any of her old obsessions in the one afternoon [in New York] we had together. Forgive me for running on so. She had many friends here, you know, and everyone has been as kind as possible and done all they could. I still can't believe it is true, that's all – and can't imagine what I am going to do with my life now.

Nadia Mandelstam to Osip Mandelstam   22 October 1938

Osia, my beloved, faraway sweetheart!

I have no words, my darling, to write this letter that you may never read, perhaps. I am writing it into empty space. Perhaps you will come back and not find me here. Then this will be all you have left to remember me by.

Osia, what a joy it was living together like children – all our squabbles and arguments, the games we played, and our love. Now I do not even look at the sky. If I see a cloud, who can I show it to?

Remember the way we brought back provisions to make our poor feasts in all the places where we pitched our tent like nomads? Remember the good taste of bread when we got it by a miracle and ate it together? And our last winter in Voronezh. Our happy poverty, and the poetry you wrote. I remember the time we were coming back once from the baths, when we bought some eggs or sausage, and a cart went by loaded with hay. It was still cold and I was freezing in my short jacket (but nothing like what we must suffer now: I know how cold you are). That day comes back to me now. I understand so clearly, and ache from the pain of it, that those winter days with all their troubles were the greatest and last happiness to be granted us in life.

My every thought is about you. My every tear and every smile is for you. I bless every day and every hour of our bitter life together, my sweetheart, my companion, my blind guide in life.

Like two blind puppies, we were, nuzzling each other and feeling so good together. And how fevered your poor head was, and how madly we frittered away the days of our life. What joy it was, and how we always knew what joy it was.

Life can last so long. How hard and long for each of us to die alone. Can this fate be for us who are inseparable? Puppies and children, did we deserve this? Did you deserve this, my angel? Everything goes on as before. I know nothing. Yet I know everything – each day and hour of your life are plain and clear to me as in a delirium.

You came to me every night in my sleep, and I kept asking what had happened, but you did not reply.

In my last dream I was buying food for you in a filthy hotel restaurant. The people with me were total strangers. When I had bought it, I realized I did not know where to take it, because I do not know where you are.

When I woke up, I said to Shura: 'Osia is dead.' I do not know whether you are still alive, but from the time of that dream, I have lost track of you. I do not know where you are. Will you hear me? Do you know how much I love you? I could never tell you how much I love you. I cannot tell you even now. I speak only to you, only to you. You are with me always, and I who was such a wild and angry one and never learned to weep simple tears – now I weep and weep and weep.

It's me: Nadia. Where are you?

Farewell.

Nadia

ENVOI

Richard Steele to his wife   *16 February 1716*

Dear Prue,
   Sober or not, I am ever yours.

ACKNOWLEDGMENTS

Thanks are due to the following copyright holders for permission to reprint extracts from:

BERG, ALBAN: Faber & Faber Ltd. and Eric Glass for *Alban Berg: Letters to his Wife*, tr. Bernard Grun. CAMPBELL, STELLA: Hubbard Solicitors & Co. for *Bernard Shaw and Mrs Patrick Campbell: Their Correspondence*, ed. Alan Dent. CARRINGTON, DORA: Random House UK Ltd. and A.P. Watt for *Carrington: Letters and Extracts from her Diary*, ed. David Garnett. CHEKHOV, ANTON: HarperCollins Publishers Ltd. for *Letters of Anton Chekhov*, tr. Michael Henry Helm and Simon Karlinsky. COLETTE, S.G.: Farrar, Straus & Giroux for *Letters from Colette*, tr. Robert Phelps. ELOÏSE: Penguin Books Ltd. for *The Letters of Eloïse and Abelard*, tr. Betty Radice (Penguin Classics, 1974) Copyright © Betty Radice, 1974. FLAUBERT, GUSTAVE: Harvard University Press for *The Letters of Gustave Flaubert*, tr. Francis Steegmuller. KAFKA, FRANZ: Secker & Warburg and Random House Inc. for *Letters to Felice*, tr. James Stern and Elizabeth Duckworth. MANSFIELD, KATHERINE: Reprinted by permission of the Society of Authors as the literary representatives of the Estate of Katherine Mansfield from the Letters of Katherine Mansfield to John Middleton Murry, ed. J.M. Murray, (1928, 1929). MOZART, WOLFGANG AMADEUS: Macmillan Press Ltd. for *The Letters of Mozart and His Family*, ed. Emily Anderson. NIN, ANAÏS: Allison & Busby Ltd., London, and Harcourt Brace & Co. for *A Literate Passion: Letters of Anaïs Nin and Henry Miller*, ed. Gunther Stuhlmann.

INDEX OF LETTER WRITERS